Angela Shelly

PRAY TO WIN!

10 Keys to Winning in Life By Being Powerful in Prayer

First paperback edition, August 2019
Book Design by Brie Digiovine
Published by Living Streams Media
www.livingstreamsmedia.com

ISBN-13: 978-0-578-54867-8

10 9 8 7 6 5 4 3 2 1

Dedication

Lord Jesus, I thank You for this privilege and for this opportunity. I dedicate this book and my life to You. Surely, You are El Roi! To my husband Eric, my best friend since our childhood - I love you. Thank you for your love and support. I pray that we forever fill our home with joy, laughter and love. To my mom and dad, thank you for teaching me strength and kindness. I love you always. To my heart-beats, Erien and Ariel, you are my sign and wonder. You are my daily inspiration. I pray that I serve you well, make you proud and lead you along straight paths.

Table of Contents

1

Almost a Casualty of War

We were on the brink of divorce. My husband had become pastor of our church and in his early years of leadership. I never imagined that I would be a pastor's wife myself and didn't know what to do or how to do it. Yet while he worked to build our church, we were failing as a family. When I reached the point that I couldn't handle it anymore, I sat him down to negotiate custody of our twin girls.

Few people knew the struggles our family was going through. Even fewer would have understood. Christians have the false perception that a pastoral family is flawless, having no idea the type of ruthless war the enemy wages against them. I for one did not.

However, before we finished negotiating all the terms of the divorce, my husband, undoubtedly under the leadings of the Holy Spirit, decided to hold a special conference at our church. If I could have skipped the entire event I would have, but feeling the need to save face I dutifully attended. Each night, I took my usual seat on the first row as the pastor's wife. My body was present, but my heart was not. I was angry, heartbroken, and borderline bitter about the past and the chain of events that had brought us to this place. And worse, it seemed I had no one to turn to or confide in. I felt alone, isolated and emotionally bankrupt.

On the second night of the conference, the guest speaker, who had no idea of our impending divorce, ministered on the love of Jesus. I reluctantly listened and was caught off guard when the minister stopped, looked right at me and said, "Jesus is going to love you. It's not based on your husband or anybody else. Jesus is going to love you!" I recognized the voice in those words. Jesus was reaching out to me. I heard Him just as clearly as if He had hijacked the preacher's voice and was talking to me face to face. Piercing my hardened heart, His words were like arrows of love. How could Jesus love me and let me go through this? I thought. But as those words penetrated my soul, I realized that was exactly what I was missing — confidence in God's love.

As the minister continued his message, I felt the defensive walls I had built around my heart begin to crack under the weight of God's love for me. My defenses had become my hiding place, my security, my shelter, and my friend. Whenever I felt the hurt of disappointment and shame, I worked to make the walls even bigger, higher, stronger. But my walls were no match for the love of God.

In the two sentences the minister spoke to me, Jesus spoke his love. He spoke joy. He spoke words of hope and maybe. Maybe my marriage wasn't over. Maybe there was a future. Maybe Jesus could save my family after all. Suddenly, I had a thought I had never had before: If Jesus promises to love me through it, maybe, just maybe we can make it. At the very least, I now had the courage to try.

Although it seemed time was standing still, the minister continued speaking to me. He said the Lord would talk to me more while I was alone that night. I hadn't heard from God in years but now I was willing to get past my emotions long enough to listen. I became slightly anxious about what the Lord would say to me, but I immediately knew just where I needed to start.

When the conference ended that night, and everyone had gone home, I slowly approached my husband and asked for a minute of his time. I looked him in the eyes and said, "I forgive you and I hope you can forgive me." He looked at me with amazement. His shoulders relaxed, and it seemed like the weight of the universe had just been lifted from his shoulders. We hugged for the first time in years. We still had a very long way to go but it was a start—even though I wasn't convinced it would work.

After getting the girls in bed for the night, I laid on the sofa and said, "Okay Lord, I'm here. What are we going to do?" Time went by. Silence. More time. More silence. I began doubting I could still hear Him after all. It had been a long time and maybe I wouldn't be able to recognize His voice. But just as I was giving up, I heard this strong, quiet whisper in my heart: "Choose differently daughter, lest you be counted as just another casualty of war."

In that single sentence, God painted a picture of my past, present, and future. He showed me not a literal death, but a separation from everything He had planned for my life. I also saw the enemy chalking up another win in having successfully divided yet another home and stealing God's purpose for another life. I saw that instead of fulfilling purpose, my life would become open to drama, chaos, and hopelessness. I saw a downward spiral, not only for me but for my children as well. The end of my marriage would be nothing new, I would be just another casualty of war. Another unsuspecting Christian succumbing to the enemy's plot to steal, kill and destroy by using unforgiveness, deceit, and destruction.

That's when I finally understood it all. My family had not only been under attack, we had been ambushed! I had been so focused on myself and my emotions that I couldn't see the bigger picture. What started out as one area of discord between my husband and I had been just the first wave of a full-fledged attack. The enemy had engaged us on all sides. We had been out maneuvered, outflanked, and undone. He had used the best weapon in his arsenal: getting us to commit fratricide by engaging in friendly fire. He used us against ourselves!

Yet, at the very moment my husband and I were pulling out our white flags in surrender, the Lord stepped in to expose the enemy's tactics. I still had free will to make my own decision, but it was as if God said, "I will not step over her will, but I will make sure she knows what she is deciding." The Lord challenged my thoughts. What if love really doesn't ever fail? What if it was partly my fault? What if I was choking my husband with the same grip of judgement I felt growing up? What if I wasn't as right as I thought I was?

As the Lord showed me the truth of the situation, I knew I had to make a choice. I could choose to stay married and work through our marital problems, allowing God the opportunity to save our family, or I could let the enemy win. I could continue to side with my emotions, wallow in self-pity, and live the rest of my life in a way I never wanted.

That night, the Lord performed spiritual open-heart surgery on me. He cut through anger and hurt like a ribcage, exposing the tender flesh of my heart. He removed the blockages of bitterness and disappointment, giving me a chance to live again. Exhausted yet hopeful for the first time in years, I finally opened my mouth and said, "OK, Jesus. You promise me this night that You will love me through this. You said you would love me. I'm going to need that love if we're going to pull this off." I knew He had already promised that, and

"He built me up every time I kneeled down."

it was me who had to get on board with what He was already doing. I didn't know where to begin, but I somehow knew prayer, conversation with God, would be essential. That night, my prayer life was officially reborn.

The next day, I began taking steps to pull my family back together. I sat down and talked to my husband. I threw away the divorce papers and started planning a new future. The turnaround wasn't easy nor was it immediate. There was a war going on for our marriage, but at least now I knew to fight.

There were times when the enemy would take his best shots at us by reminding us of our past. He specializes in creating those emotional wounds and then throws steady punches right on them. The enemy has a "no holds barred" policy. He doesn't fight fair and he plays to win. I knew none of this at the time. Being a pastor's wife, I felt as if I had no one I could trust to turn to. So, I ran to my prayer closet, closed the doors, and fell to my knees. Tears streaming, snot dripping, I cried, "Lord Jesus! Help me! You promised! You promised You would love me! I don't know how to do this. I don't know how to do anything beyond what I've been doing and clearly that doesn't work. How do I fight?" Years of hurt all the way back from childhood caused panic and confusion to pour out with each tear. There was a pattern. Every time my husband and I made progress in restoring our relationship, the enemy showed up to push me right back into despair. I was scared my future would look like my past. The enemy fought me with his weapon of fear. The only weapon I knew was prayer. And it was just the weapon I would need.

During those times of brokenness on my closet floor, Jesus revealed His love to me more and more. He built me up every time I kneeled down. It was there that I learned His voice and learned how to fight. He schooled me in the weapon of praise. He gave me the weapon of joy. He taught me to lean on Him for everything. Then God showed me His own strategy.

Driving the girls to school one morning after yet another disagreement with my husband, I was asking the Lord to please take this fight from me. I was tired of fighting, battling, crying. I wanted this to be over, enough was enough. Then He spoke His strategy almost audibly to my heart: "My will is that you get victory in this war, not deliverance from it."

I didn't know it at the time, but those times on my knees were where the battles were won or lost. Every time I prayed, I won. There was where He made my heart fixed, rooted, and firmly dependent on Him. There He covered me with the Kevlar armor of His love. He taught me that people are people, all works in progress. None of us have yet arrived, myself being no exception.

A year went by. We were having more good days than bad. But one morning, my husband and I had another big fight. I stopped speaking to him and was not interested in doing so. I felt the temptation of putting up walls begin to creep back in. And as had become my custom, I ran to the Lord about it. On my knees praying and crying, He said, "Daughter, stand up. You're much stronger than this." Shocked at His response, I said, "I am?! Do you see me right now? Uhm, I'm pretty upset!" But in obedience, I stood up. I looked inside my heart and found while my emotions were stirred up, my heart was safe. Look-y there! I thought, because my thoughts apparently have a southern accent as well, here I stand, unharmed! What would have sent me into a panic spiral before no longer had the power to do so. I was mad, but I was still OK. I was beginning to walk in the victory He had promised. I got so excited that I couldn't even be mad anymore. I was winning the war!

From that point forward, each day got better than the next. Not because it was uneventful, but because I was fortified. Kevlar covered. Bulletproof.

This book isn't just about praying, it's about praying to win. It's about giving you the ammunition, weaponry, and skillset of developing a prayer life so powerful that you walk in victory in every area of your life. ***Because we don't just pray, we pray to win!*** ○⚮

"When your why is big enough
you will find your how."
- LES BROWN

2 What's Your Why?

There are two extremes in prayer. There are prayers we release to heaven like helium-filled balloons from an old birthday party, half-filled with air and no sense of direction. Casual prayers of no real consequence. The ones we pray in the car asking Jesus to help us get the kids to school on time, but 10 minutes later, there we are — signing kids in at the front desk because we missed the bell, and we aren't even surprised. We knew that prayer was a long shot when we said it. Short of God transporting us through time and space, there is no way to make a twenty-minute ride to school happen in five minutes.

And, there are prayers we say because our very lives are at stake—or at least it feels like it. When cancer hits, when layoffs occur, or when your child is diagnosed with a terminal illness. These two extremes mark the difference between when you think you know how to pray and when you know that you do—and conversely, when you do not.

I remember the moment I realized I didn't know how to pray, at least not effectively. I was young and happily married but still found myself battling depression and suicidal thoughts that had plagued me since childhood. It came to a tipping point when doctors told me that my body was too broken to have kids of my own, not without significant medical intervention. In the days that followed I realized quickly that my problems were bigger than my prayer life. I flat out needed a miracle.

My prayer life back then looked a lot like the Hokey-Pokey dance. So desperate for results, I did all kinds of "Christianese" stuff:

I put my faith foot in,
I took my whole self out.
I put my hope hand in,
And I shook it all about.
I did the hokey-pokey and I turned myself around...
Was this what praying was all about?

No, not at all! I simply just didn't know any better. And honestly, I hadn't taken the time to learn. I wanted the results of an effective prayer life, but I didn't want to put in the effort. I wanted it to come easily and instantaneously. And as pregnancies turned into miscarriages, as months of waiting became years of heartbreak, my ignorance caused my faith to become faint and then fail. But God always causes us to triumph in Jesus Christ. As I type, my twin girls just turned 9 years old and are a testimony of both the love of God and the effectiveness of prayer.

God is true to His Word. He promises that if we ask Him for wisdom, He gives it liberally (James 1:5). There is absolutely a skillful way to pray—an effective way to pray. If your desire is to know how to pray and see God's work in your life, then I have got keys to share with you! My prayer is that through this book, you will be guided into developing an effective prayer life of your own and that goes hand in hand with living an effective Christian life.

As the saying goes, it's hard to build a shelter in the middle of a storm. I pray you find this book in the blue-sky times of your life. If you are in the middle of a storm, it may be harder, but we will build anyhow. Are you ready? Let's go!

JAMES 1:5 NKJV
5 If any of you lacks wisdom, let him ask of God, who gives to all liberally and without reproach, and it will be given to him."

Prayer Is an Essential Part of Your Relationship with God

Have you ever had a relationship with somebody you really liked, but their track record with you was flaky? Meaning sometimes that person showed up and sometimes he didn't, and you never knew exactly which you were going to get? I'm willing to hypothetically bet you may even really like that person, but in times of crisis, his name is not the one you call on for help. Your experience with him tells you that you simply can't count on him to come through.

If we pray, but we never quite know which of our prayers will be answered and which ones won't, eventually our experience will tell us the same thing about God.

Even if we won't readily admit it, our actions sell us out and we find ourselves not trusting God.

Distrust takes many forms. There's the form where we stop praying altogether. The form where we pray but we make sure we keep a backup plan just in case God doesn't show up. And there's the form of distrust where we know what He is asking us to do, but we don't do it. We decide it is too risky or that it won't work. There's even the form of distrust that sounds like this: "Lord, if it's Your will, then I will be healed of this disease."

Now, that last one is the most deceptive of all because it sounds like complete trust! But it's often our religious cop out, and what we really mean is: "Lord, I don't know if I trust You to show up, so I won't get my hopes up too high."

Back to the friend. Now, what if your friend wasn't flaky? What if instead he was the most dependable, reliable, honest, and upfront person you ever met? Would that friend not be your closest of friends—the one you knew had your back, regardless of what was going on?

What if that's what a relationship with Jesus was like instead? Where you knew every time you prayed, He heard you, and He responded. Where you knew there was nothing you couldn't talk to Him about. Where you knew He loved you and had your back every single time. Trust would be developed; a real relationship would grow. Well my friends, that's exactly the point. It's a relationship.

The more time I spend with any person, the more I come to know how to talk to them in a way that's pleasing to them. The more time I spend with Jesus, the better I get at knowing how to talk to Him, the better I get speaking His language, and the more effective my prayers are. As we study how Jesus lived, we become more familiar with His ways and His will. The more I learn what Jesus taught, said, and did, the better I become at knowing His voice, so I will not follow the voice of a stranger. John 10:4-5 paraphrase.

Spoiler Alert! There is no shortcut to effective prayer. There is no 10-step plan to a having a more effective prayer life. The main thing is spending time alone with Jesus, in prayer and in His Word. *"But Angela! You said the purpose of this book is to guide me in having a powerful prayer life! And you said there are 10 keys!"* It is and it will, but it's based on the Word of God, time spent with God, and obedience to God. Let me repeat that: effective prayer is based on the Word of God, time spent with God, and obedience to God.

The keys detailed in this book will give you guidance and insight for being effective in your prayer and the time you spend with God but let me be clear— there is NO substitute for actually spending time in His presence and developing a relationship with Him yourself. When we learn how to pray effectively, we eliminate our failures in praying in error that cause us to doubt God and we invite the very presence of God into our lives and our circumstances.

JOHN 10:4-5 NKJV
4 And when he brings out his own sheep, he goes before them; and the sheep follow him, for they know his voice. 5 Yet they will by no means follow a stranger, but will flee from him, for they do not know the voice of strangers."

Know Your Why

I'm positive, whether knowingly or not, you're reading this book for a reason. Ask yourself. Better yet, ask the Lord — why. Why do you need to be able to pray effectively? This is important to know because you will be challenged in it. When you know your why, you will persist. In the chapter "Almost A Casualty of War," I had a very strong why and it propelled me forward in prayer to a greater degree than I had ever had before. But bad situations aren't the only reasons to develop a prayer life. Let me share a few of mine.

01. I've learned I don't know nearly as much as I think I do. *I need His wisdom.*

02. I've learned I don't have nearly as much control as I think I do. *I need His care.*

03. I've learned I am not nearly as smart as I thought I was. *I need His infinite knowledge.*

04. I've learned I am not nearly as strong as I believed I was. *I need His protection.*

05. I've learned I was not nearly as put together as I let people believe I was. *I need His covering.*

06. *Lastly, I learned that without Him, I can do nothing, but through him I can do all things!*

Why Pray?

Why do we pray? I mean, really, why? Is it because we are taught we "ought" to pray? Is it because we feel obligated, as if we are doing God a favor by spending time with Him? Do we pray because we need something from God or want God to do something on our behalf?

I'm not questioning your reasoning, but it is important to know the true why behind your prayers. God is a God of truth. We can fool ourselves, but I am sure we cannot fool Him. What I love about Him is that He knows us inside and out and loves us anyway. He loves us when our motives are right and when they aren't. So, we don't have to say, "I can't talk to Jesus until my heart's right." Truth is, it's only in Jesus that our hearts can ever be right. If there is no other place you can be honest, be honest with Him.

So back to the question: Why do we pray? In developing an effective prayer life, there is only one answer (aka root cause, for my fellow engineer geeks) and that is this: To know Him. It's the point. It's why He came to redeem us, so that we can be free to fellowship with God again. It's the real reason we pray.

When Jesus walked this earth, He spent time in prayer, significant time in prayer, because His mission was to be the expressed image of God the Father on the earth. To show His love. To show it and to express it, He had to know it. And where did that knowing come from? You guessed it, time spent in prayer on His knees, talking it out, and on His feet, walking it out.

Walking Out Your Why

Is it possible to have all our prayers answered? It most certainly is—Jesus did. OK, yes, I hear you already, "Angela, of course He did, He's Jesus! For crying out loud." But Jesus never made His success a secret. He came to be our example, our go-by for how to be victorious in God. He said in John 16:23 that whatever we ask the Father in His name, He will give it. That sounds to me like a weighty promise. But we will come back to this. The initial point here is that prayer is designed to be effective. Even recalling the Old Testament, you don't read often of prayers that weren't answered.

The disciples saw this remarkable consistency with Jesus. He prayed, and the Father answered. Every time. So, what was Jesus doing differently? Jesus said, "I only do that which I hear the Father do... I only say that which I hear the Father say." Let's draw a parallel of that.

At age nine, my twins can wear my name out asking for stuff. "Mommy, can I this? Mommy, can we that? Mommy, when this?" You get the point. They find no shortage of things to ask for or places to go. And it's fine, they're nine. But I tell you what, my day would be filled with a lot fewer questions and their day would be filled with a whole lot fewer no's if instead of bombarding me with their bright (not so bright) ideas, they simply asked this question first: "Mommy, what are we doing today? What plans do you have for us?"

What if whenever their "great not so great" ideas sparked, they came back and added, "I was thinking about doing this, what do you think, Mommy?" Oh, what a smooth sailing day that would be. The entire day, me and the girls on the same page, doing what needed to be done as well as having fun too. Well, that's pretty much what Jesus did. He heard from the Father and conducted himself accordingly. We must be willing to let go of our agendas if we want our prayers to be effective.

Can I share a story with you? It's the biggest lesson I ever learned about letting go of my agenda for God's plan.

"Dear God, not again," I prayed. Walking to the bathroom, I remembered my last miscarriage. How, after 11 weeks of pregnancy, the doctors found no heartbeat and surgically removed what remained in my womb. I recalled the shame, the hope lost, the disappointment. I recalled the anger of having hoped so long and so hard just to have it end so harshly. Tears falling, I got to the bathroom and sat down. Now, here I was, with blood-stained underwear, facing a miscarriage again.

I don't know which hurt worse: losing another pregnancy or losing my faith. In that moment, I lost both. I had trusted, prayed, and believed I would see God fix this for me. After all, I had been a faithful Christian since I was nineteen. I loved Jesus. He had healed me from the pain of losing my brother to suicide years before. He had blessed me tremendously by putting my high school sweetheart turned husband, Eric, and me together. So why had God abandoned me in the very thing I desired most — a family?

Short on faith and low on hope, I tried to persevere, but things got even worse. I found the best doctors and went through several tests and procedures of various types and intensities. What they found shocked me.

I had three major birth defects: half a uterus, only one ovary, and the fallopian tube was blocked. Doctors couldn't explain how I had even gotten pregnant. Lab tests also showed I had a condition causing my blood to clot in the womb — the likely cause of my miscarriages. I literally needed a miracle.

Hope Lost

I spent the next few years coming to grips with those results. How could I, the one my mom always said would have a house full of puppies and kids, be facing a life without children at all? Why would God let this be my story?

Being in my late twenties, I watched all, and I do mean all, of my friends have happy, healthy babies. I was torn between being genuinely excited for them and equally sad for me. Why them and not me—not us? Eric wanted children just as badly as I did. He acted like our marriage was all he needed but facing a future without children is a hard pill for anybody to swallow. After all, reproductively, he was fully functional. I was a reproductive mess.

Years passed, and the feeling of disappointment dulled. Believing Jesus loved me, even though it didn't feel like He did, I got the courage to try in-vitro fertilization. Doctors said it was our only option; Eric and I went ahead full force.

We aggressively searched for doctors in a bigger city and found one with accolades from patients all across the country. Jackpot! We began the in-vitro regimen immediately. We got on a set schedule, Eric giving me shots of one hormone in the morning and another at night. I spent more time researching on the Internet
than doing my job developing software. I became obsessively focused on the process. Doctors also put me on daily blood-thinning shots to correct the clotting situation. All I needed to do was get pregnant. This was my time, and this was going to work.

After six weeks of manipulating my reproductive system, the doctor implanted one fertilized embryo and sent me home to recover.

And wait.

And wait.

And wait.

Finally, three weeks later, we went to the doctor's office to take the pregnancy test. All day, my cell phone was never more than two inches away, and I jumped every time it rang. Around 2:30 that afternoon the call came. "Not pregnant," the nurse said.

My husband had heard the news first and rushed to my job to pick me up, knowing I would be devastated. Fist pounding the dashboard in the car, I shouted, "That's it, Jesus! I give up! I can't do this anymore. This hoping and believing and trusting You just ends in disappointment. And You don't even care! You don't care! This isn't even hard for You to do, but You choose not to help me!"

Days led to months, months led to years. I attended church regularly, but my heart wasn't there. One thought: He doesn't care about me, so why should I care about Him?—raced through my mind constantly. Every time I saw a pregnant stranger, I felt it simply served as a reminder that I was the one NOT loved by God. So, I stopped attending church altogether. What was the point?

Letting it Go

I don't recall how I ended up in church at a Thursday evening Bible study, but I remember sitting quietly in the back, half-heartedly listening, yet desperately searching for an answer. The minister read what Jesus said about it being easier for a camel to get through the eye of the needle than a rich man to enter the kingdom of Heaven. In that moment, I saw my rich self sitting there as if I had something to be whining about. I still had my husband who made me laugh every day, I had an awesome career, and I had a great dog; you can never overestimate a great dog. But I hadn't been able to see it because all I looked at was what I didn't have. In that moment, I made a decision. "Lord Jesus," I prayed, "if I never have kids, if it were always just Eric and me, I'll still serve You."

Determined to be grateful for all I did have, I began to heal emotionally and spiritually. It took a few years, but in time, Jesus rebuilt my trust in Him and restored my joy, peace, and excitement about life. I was living again!

A few years later — seven years from the first miscarriage, in fact — my pastor pulled me aside and said, "Angela, it's time to give it one more try." Wait, what?! Was he smoking those funny cigarettes? I thought. Jesus and I had worked way too hard to pull me out of that devastation, and I was in no hurry to jump back in. "You don't know what I've been through!" I replied. But he insisted it was time, and in my heart, I hoped he was right. My husband agreed to give it one last try. This time, I just went to the local doctor. Either Jesus was going to do this, or He wasn't.

We went through the entire process again: the schedules, the shots, the appointments, the waiting. Doctors said my fertility levels were very low, and this would be the last time my body could handle the procedure. So we threw caution to the wind and implanted three embryos. It took six long, arduous weeks, but at last the test results came back. We were pregnant!

Having It All

To describe that as a happy day is to describe the Grand Canyon as a little valley. My husband and I celebrated, but cautiously. Given my past, we were still on edge. I had gotten to this point before and miscarried. I needed to see the ultrasound and hear the heartbeat before I would allow myself to get too excited.

Exactly one day before the scheduled ultrasound, I had a massive bleeding episode at work. In the same moment the bleeding started, a knowing peace came over me, reminding me to keep trusting Jesus. I called my husband, and he reassured me that the Lord was with us. I went home that afternoon to take it easy. I walked out on my porch, looked up at the sky, and I cried, "Jesus! Son of David! Have mercy on me!" It was all in His hands, and I was trusting in Him. Refusing to let the past overwhelm me, we kept the ultrasound appointment. Hands sweating, I lay there as the doctor scanned my belly. Eric and I held our breaths. And then we saw them ... two little pea-sized things and two little heartbeats. My half uterus carried not one baby, but two!

Today, my twins are thriving, and they are the absolute loves of my life. I never dreamed I would have twins, and now I couldn't imagine my life without them.

To this day, I believe that if I had not been so stubborn and insistent about having children when I wanted to have them and had I simply asked God and trusted His timing and process, the seven years of disappointment and heartache I went through could have been avoided. My heart wasn't open to His direction. I wanted what I wanted, and I wanted it right then. And as long as I elevated my own plans above His plans, I got nowhere fast. But God's plans and timing are always perfect! My husband and I are able to provide for our girls now in ways we never could have in an earlier time and space in our lives. Not only financially, but also in the giving of ourselves to them as parents. My prayer life, my walk with God, is essential in not only my well-being, but for my kids as well. God's plan and timing is so much better than if I had had it my way!

PHILIPPIANS 4:6 NLT

6 Don't worry about anything; instead, pray about everything. Tell God what you need, and thank him for all he has done.

Listen Twice as Much as You Speak

In the book, "Prepared for a Purpose" by Antoinette Tuff, she talks about her approach to her personal time in prayer. Her book about her experience being used by God to stop an active shooter situation at a school in Georgia provided me with some very helpful guidance to me in my own prayer time. She simply said that when she prayed, she made sure she was quiet and listened twice as long as the time she spent talking. That was an "a-ha" moment for me! That's not to say we need to get out our timers and be literal about that. The takeaway is the realization that not only is prayer bi-directional, but that it's far more important for us to hear what the Lord is saying than it is for us to tell Him about all our problems and requests. He knows that already. And certainly, the Bible instructs us to make our request known to God (Philippians 4:6). But if I were to ask you the question, "How do I get from Nashville, Tennessee to Austin, Texas?" the time I spent asking

"It takes practice putting down what we want to hear so that we can really listen."

the question is far shorter than the time it takes to hear the answer. Sometimes, we need to stop praying and start listening. When we make it a practice to be quiet in prayer so that we can listen, it becomes easier to still our minds from all the noise and distractions. Yes, it takes practice.

It takes practice putting down what we want to hear so that we can really hear. There are times when I am too emotionally connected to a situation to really hear what the Lord is saying about it clearly. Sometimes we want something so badly that our hearts become like a trampoline, bouncing back what the Lord is saying instead of taking it in. I wanted children so badly and prayed so hard about it that I couldn't hear Him saying, "Yes, but not right now." But thanks be to God, He works all things together for our good. Amen!

Even though it seems to be the most difficult to listen to God's direction when you want something the most, it's often when we need to hear His voice with an open heart the most. As the saying goes, if you want it bad, you'll get it bad. Resist the urge to let your emotions out-weigh your relationship with God. As my pastor says, "Wear it loosely," referring to the things in this life. The Lord says in Jeremiah 29:11 NIV, "For I know the plans I have for you," declares the Lord, "plans to prosper you and not to harm you, plans to give you hope and a future." We can trust His plans, but we must choose to trust them first.

JEREMIAH 29:11 NIV
"For I know the plans I have for you," declares the Lord, "plans to prosper you and not to harm you, plans to give you hope and a future."

"It is not the lie that passes through the mind,
but the lie that sinks in and settles in it,
that does the hurt."
- FRANCIS BACON

3 Let's Be Honest

The human mind is a clever thing. It is so tenacious with protecting and defending itself that it will pull off remarkable feats to do so. Let me explain what I mean. A few years ago, I attended a leadership workshop where the speaker talked about Micro-Inequities. That's just a fancy way of describing how people show internal bias to situations, conversations, and personal encounters. That's my unofficial take, anyway. During that workshop, the speaker shared how the human brain literally just makes stuff up. It tries to fill in gaps when it doesn't understand something about a situation, or person, or concept. Instead of admitting it doesn't know, its tendency (in the vain of self-preservation) will jump to conclusions and then present those conclusions to your conscious as fact. It will defend your decisions and make excuses. It will self-justify. In other words, it's a mess!

I remember the day I realized just how right he was. It was close to 4:30 in the afternoon and I was debating whether or not to leave work or to finish up a few things first. I called my husband to make sure he had picked up the girls from school and didn't mind me being late getting home. But he didn't answer. So, I called right back, still no answer. My mind immediately did what the speaker had told me about, but I didn't realize it.

My thoughts started spinning trying to figure out why he didn't answer. Then I concluded to myself, He must have overslept and forgot to get the girls and now he doesn't want to answer the phone because he knows I'll be upset. Yep, that's what happened, I was convinced of it. I sat there, based on this narrative I had going in my head, and called him repeatedly for fifteen more minutes. Finally, time was running out, so I said to myself, Let me leave work now if I'm going to get to school before after school care closes.

I left work, hopped in the car, and started driving. And I was hot! I had so much to say when my husband finally called me back and I was ready to let him have it. Then about three minutes into my drive, he called. Now Eric is always trying to trick me and likes to play this game telling me he forgot to pick up the girls. (Back story, he forgot to get them one time and it would appear that I have a problem letting that go.) I blurted, "You got the kids?" He replied, "No, I thought you were picking them up today." Since I had already worked myself into frenzy, I responded, "No! Remember you said this morning…"

Before I could even finish, I heard the girls laughing in the background, talking to each other. I changed mid-sentence and said, "Wait. Why didn't you answer my phone call?!" He said, "Oh, I was in the bank and gave the girls my phone to play with while I handled a few things."

Yep, I had made the whole thing up in my head. That conference guy was right. In my head I didn't know the situation so instead of admitting that, my brain concocted this whole scenario up instead. Then serving as judge and jury, I convicted my husband of not picking up our kids and making me scramble across town. Guilty! I had already sentenced Him to cold stares and an evening of pure silence. But, I had made the whole thing up in my head and then acted on it like it was Gospel truth. Lord have mercy.

And we do this more often than we realize. And it is critical that we be more mindful of when we are making stuff up. Why? Because the human mind, in its attempt to defend and justify you, will deceive and distort the truth.

By now I'm sure you're asking yourself, what on earth does this have to do with prayer? Well, because the mind has this propensity to "make stuff up," we need help to even know when and where we've erroneously filled in the gaps with false information in our lives. False information about who we are, false information about our thoughts and behaviors. God sent the Holy Spirit to be that help. He is the Spirit of truth and He helps us see the truth, so we can come to a place of honesty. In prayer, honesty is essential. And if we're not honest with ourselves, how can

"Effective prayer comes from a loving, honest heart."

we be honest with God? God already knows the truth, but under the narrative of false information, we often create spiritual barriers by trying to hide parts of our lives from Him. The Holy Spirit is a gentleman, He will not overstep your walls, you must invite Him in. But it is the Holy Spirit who enables us to talk to God about the real us, and He allows us to know our real selves – and how we all need a Savior.

My husband called me judgmental for years, but I didn't see it at all. I told him he was being judgmental for calling me judgmental. I would get so mad and step right into my self-righteousness declaring what I thought was right and what I thought was wrong, according to the world of me. It took a series of life events before the Holy Spirit could show me through conversations and situations that Eric was right, I was judgmental. I had a narrative in my head about what should be and shouldn't be, lacking compassion and understanding of other people. Jesus Himself had a few choice words to say about being that way.

> *Do not judge and criticize and condemn others, so*
> *that you may not be judged and criticized and*
> *condemned yourselves.*
> **MATTHEW 7:1 AMP**

Suffice it to say, once the Lord revealed that to me, I knew I had to change. I did not want to be on the other side of that stick! Not only for myself, but He showed me that I wouldn't be able to pray effectively for myself, my husband, or anyone else as long as I was also putting myself in the judgment seat for that person. Effective prayer comes from a loving, honest heart. Faith works by love and without it, our prayers won't get very far. That's one reason why there isn't a ten-step plan or an exact recipe to follow when it comes to prayer. It's fluid, it's alive, and it works by the principles in God's Word.

"For [if we are] in Christ Jesus, neither circumcision nor uncircumcision counts for anything, but only faith activated and energized and expressed and working through love."
GALATIANS 5:6 AMPC

The Power of Honesty

Our willingness to be brutally honest with ourselves invites Truth to show us exactly what is hindering our prayers. There are hindrances like unforgiveness, sin, not being grateful, and more. You may be thinking, "Angela, I don't know if I'm ready for that." Or you may even be thinking, "Oh, phew, I'm good with this one. I have NO problem being honest with myself or God." Good! Take both of those statements to the Lord and allow Him to work both sides of the spectrum. If you think for some reason that you're not ready to be nakedly honest before the Lord, talk to Him about it and ask Him to help you. He knows exactly how to nurture and guide you. And I promise He won't hurt you. Now sometimes the truth may hurt our emotions, but it's a hurt that results in healing. If, however, you're thinking you got this honesty thing nailed tight, then I ask that you take that to Him as well and ask Him, "Lord, is there anything in me that I'm not letting you deal with? If so, I welcome You to reveal that and begin to deal with me in that area." It's not about where we are or where we are not, it's about being effective in prayer and getting results!

When my husband and I were considering divorce, I didn't need my trickster brain swelling me with pride, I needed the truth and God's help! And honestly, no pun on this topic intended, the same areas the Lord dealt with me personally about in prayer were the same areas hindering the full restoration of our marriage. Funny how that works.

Let me throw in a bit of a bonus plug here. As you pray about your situations, especially as they relate to other people — whether that be your spouse, your children, your family, your friends, or even the people at work — I guarantee you will discover that the Lord will begin by working on you first. Yep, through all of our insights on what is wrong with other people, the Lord almost always deals with us first. Oh, how I used to hate that part.

"You hypocrite, first get the beam of timber out of your own eye, and then you will see clearly to take the tiny particle out of your brother's eye."

MATTHEW 7:5 AMPC

I'd go before the Lord, telling Him all about what my husband did or didn't do, what my parents did or didn't do, co-workers, whoever. What I heard from God in response were faults in me. And as I became more forgiving, understanding, supporting, and encouraging to my husband, the more I saw my husband change as well. And the Holy Spirit came to my aid every time I needed Him to.

I remember one day specifically, me and my husband were going out to run errands and I asked him a simple question. Well, my husband can have a very biting tongue and he replied in his usual sarcastic way and that day it really rubbed me the wrong way. Especially so because it was during the time we were beginning the relationship rebuilding and the tension between us was still pretty high. Instead of retaliating, I just walked to my bathroom and cried out, "Now Lord, don't nobody want to have to deal with his mouth all the time, not ALL the time." (My grammar seems to take a back seat when I'm angry.) I stayed right there in that bathroom for at least ten minutes. I put some praise music on to force myself to a place of praise. As my emotions settled, I was able to refocus on what I was praying for in our marriage.

When I was ready, I forgave him in my heart and walked out of the bathroom ready to proceed with the day. As soon as Eric saw me, he said, "Hey, I'm really sorry about what I just said." I laughed to myself and said, "The Holy Spirit just got on to you, didn't He?" Eric replied, "Maybe!" and we laughed together. I was so grateful that the Lord stood up for me in that moment without me having to say a word. That's when I knew God had my back and I really was going to be OK. Even to this day, I tear up thinking about how God loves us just that much that He works on our behalf in even the little things. That's the result of honesty and relationship.

The more we walk in honest prayer, the more we know beyond a shadow of doubt that prayer is a safe place, we will talk to the Lord about our deepest, darkest secrets. You can (and should) confess your wrongs, your hurts, your past, your present — everything to God. He is our Creator and He knows exactly how to forgive, heal, restore, mend, and develop you. He's the best friend you will ever, ever have. I've told God things I haven't told anybody else. He didn't judge me for it, He helped me through it. But it starts with trusting Him enough to be honest with Him.

Having an Honest Perspective of Prayer

"For now we are looking in a mirror that gives only a dim (blurred) reflection [of reality as in a riddle or enigma], but then [when perfection comes] we shall see in reality and face to face! Now I know in part (imperfectly), but then I shall know and understand fully and clearly, even in the same manner as I have been fully and clearly known and understood [by God]."
1 CORINTHIANS 13:12 AMP

Isn't it terrific that through prayer we have the opportunity to have conversation with the Almighty God, the author

MATTHEW 13:5-6
so if anyone of you is lacking in wisdom, let him keep asking god, for he gives generously to all and without reproaching, and it will be given him.

and the finisher of our faith, the God Who loves us so much that He sent His only son Jesus to be the atonement of our sins so that we can come before His throne of grace with boldness? I get so excited about that! Through prayer we have the opportunity to get to know and talk to Him and Him with us—and us with ourselves. Our Creator knows us even better than we know ourselves. This is where we really get the honest truth about who we really are. In that light and with that perspective, what fools we would be to say, "I would spend time praying this morning, but I'm just too busy. He understands."

Friends, let's be very clear. I'm sure I've said it before and I can't promise this is the last time I'll say it again—prayer isn't for God, it's for us. We are the ones in need of Him, not the other way around. He is the giver of life, of hope, joy, strength, love. I don't know about you, but I need that every day. I need His wisdom every day. Our brains will mislead us into thinking that we have everything under control. They will fill us with arrogance, confidence, and a false security that we got it all figured out. Well, while our brains can be unreliable, God's Word says in Proverbs 3:5-6 AMPC, that if we acknowledge Him in all our ways, (that is, if we trust in, adhere to/obey, and rely on Him) He will direct our paths. That's what prayer does, it puts us in a place of acknowledging Him, it puts us in a place of surrendering our will to His will, knowing that we can trust Him. And if we do this daily, I guarantee His Word will perform, and I'll take that guarantee any day!

There are so many reasons to pray every day. To spend

time in His presence every day. But I can tell you this, not praying daily or on a regular, frequent basis will not result in the promises of Proverbs 3:5-6.

I'm just going to put it on the table. The kingdom of God is not something we can take or leave - or even treat our Christian walk with Christ as something to be added to our lives. It is to be the cornerstone foundation of everything concerning us. Sometimes we treat our opportunity to walk with God as something we can pick up when we hit hard times or put down when it's inconvenient. Not at all. In Matthew 13, Jesus describes what the kingdom of God is like. He said, "It's like a man who finds a treasure in a field, then goes off to sell all that he has and buys that field." It's not a "just a little bit of effort" life. It's an "all that you have" life! And life is lived daily. Prayer is about having this honest perspective, not a religious ritual.

A word of caution. Being honest doesn't mean being disrespectful or treating God with too much familiarity. The fear of the Lord is the beginning of wisdom, Proverbs says. We always need to remember Who we are talking to in prayer, but that doesn't mean we can't be blunt. It just means remember not to think more highly of yourself as His creation than we ought to and conversely not to think any less.

PROVERBS 3:5-6 AMPC
5 Lean on, trust in, and be confident in the Lord with all your heart and mind and do not rely on your own insight or understanding. 6 In all your ways know, recognize, and acknowledge Him, and He will direct and make straight and plain your paths.

MATTHEW 13:44 AMP
44 "The kingdom of heaven is like a [very precious] treasure hidden in a field, which a man found and hid again; then in his joy he goes and sells all he has and buys that field [securing the treasure for himself].

4 Because He Said So.

As a child of the 80s, the infamous words, "Because I said so" rang from house to house. You knew when your parents uttered those words, you'd better quit asking and start doing. You might have heard these words when you're arguing with your siblings or when you asked to go somewhere, and your parents said, "No." In the 80s and before, we all had the street light rule. You could play outside all day, but you had better be home before the street lights came on. Should you dare to ask why, the answer was almost always, "Because I said so." And if you knew what was good for you, that was the end of the conversation.

It's a phrase almost every parent at some point in time says. Not because they don't want to explain — well, sometimes it is — but most often it's because they know you won't understand the explanation.

Yet we often have the expectation that the LORD owes us an explanation to His instructions before we obey them. Sometimes He offers us those explanations, and sometimes He doesn't. That's why obedience must be mixed with reverential fear and faith. We do what He tells us to do, "Because He said so."

Just like we knew back in the day that when those street lights came on, it didn't matter what we were doing or how much fun we were having, it was time to get home. That's the same attitude we should have when it comes to obeying what the Lord tells us to do. It doesn't matter if we feel like it or if it's inconvenient or uncomfortable. We simply must obey. Why? Because He said so. Remember, His instructions are for our benefit, not His. God is well, with or without us. When we are disobedient, we hurt ourselves and potentially those we are divinely connected to.

An Inconvenient Truth

Not too long ago, my husband took the twins to attend a birthday party. It felt like I hadn't been home alone the entire summer and I was pretty excited. I had all kinds of fun planned! When they left, I ordered a pizza, got a blanket, put on my pajamas, and looked for a good movie to watch. This was my version of a party: peace, quiet, and a good show. Moms out there know just how thrilling a four-hour break can be.

Since I don't watch movies often, I scrolled through iTunes to see what was out. As I scrolled through, I came across a spy movie that I had been wanting to see. Years before, I read the book and found it very intriguing. But when the movie was released it got poor reviews. I didn't see any other movie worth my $4.99 so once the pizza arrived, I rented it, ready to enjoy.

Not two minutes in, the Holy Spirit started nudging me to turn it off. I suddenly felt uneasy and convicted about watching it. Not understanding why, I began debating and reasoning that surely it was ok. After all, it was just a spy movie, nothing illicit. Yes, it may have some "R" rated content, but I figured I would just fast forward past that, no big deal.

I adjusted my comfortable position on the sofa trying to get cozy, but it was my spirit that was uneasy. "I mean, people watch spy movies all the time, surely it's okay." I continued trying to talk myself out of my inner conviction. Five minutes into the movie, I had managed to watch the introduction credits and ballerina dancing on stage. That's when I heard the Lord impress upon me that this movie had more evil in it than I was aware. He reminded me that there really is no middle ground. Either the movie was made for good or it was made for evil. That sounds a bit extreme, but it's still the truth. Even though I really wanted to watch that movie, I remembered that there is only the Kingdom of God or the Kingdom of darkness. One of those two kingdoms had influenced the movie, and the Lord reassured me that this one was not of His.With that, I turned the movie off and turned to some animal doctor show.

I knew the Lord wasn't trying to keep me from enjoying my afternoon off. He was being a protective Father and letting me know that the movie was not created for my good. I don't know specifically why I couldn't watch that movie, but He had basically said, "Because I said so," and it was all up to me whether I would be home before those street lights came on or not.

"What does all this have to do with prayer?" you might ask. We know that effective prayer consists of bi-directional communication. But what we do with that communication makes all the difference!

If I manufactured a car, I would know exactly what the engine needs to run, how fast it can go, how fast it should go, how to keep it looking and running its best. I might have put in special features like anti-lock brakes or auto-assisted driving. Or if I made a Tesla, maybe there is no engine at all. However, the person who bought my car would need the owner's manual or a very long talk with me as the manufacturer. Sure, he or she may be able to figure out how to drive the car, but he might not ever know how to use all the features. Consequently, the owner may never realize the full potential.

Prayer is one of the main ways we communicate with our Manufacturer. And He gives us the instructions for how to operate us as the vehicle He created. Well, what happens if I don't do what the Manufacturer tells me to do? What happens if He tells me that my engine needs gasoline, but I put in vinegar? What happens if He tells me I need electricity, but I never plug it in? My car won't do what it's supposed to, that's for sure!

It isn't out of some legalistic constraint that the Manufacturer said to only use gasoline in my car. He knew how my car was designed. And if I go put in vinegar instead, it will damage my vehicle.

That's what disobedience does. It causes us to get results we don't want — both in prayer and in life. As we understand that prayer is an opportunity to consult with our Manufacturer, we begin to see how vitally important it is for our effectiveness in life. Let's look at some of the unwanted results disobedience brings:

1. Disobedience Makes Us Sin Conscious

Whenever I got caught doing what my mom told me not to do, I felt ashamed and awkward around her for a while. So much more when I knowingly do something that I know God is not pleased with. And the enemy will try to use that to bring about guilt and shame. I begin dwelling on the fact that I've messed up and start thinking that maybe God is mad at me. Or maybe I become so ashamed that I

1 JOHN 1:9 NLT,
"But if we confess our sins to him, he is faithful and just to forgive us our sins and to cleanse us from all wickedness."

don't talk to anybody about it, much less God. Thus, guilt and shame work together against me, keeping me from praying and avoiding His presence. Until I bring myself to confess that sin before God and ask for His forgiveness, the illusion of guilt and shame remain and hinder me from praying. Therefore, being sin conscious becomes an actual hindrance to not just the effectiveness of my prayer life, but my desire to pray altogether.

We all sin, we all make mistakes. All of us. Praise be to God, He has freely given us grace and mercy every time we come before Him. Confess those sins and turn away from them. I John 1:9 NLT promises, "But if we confess our sins to him, he is faithful and just to forgive us our sins and to cleanse us from all wickedness."

The turning away part is important. It does me and my mom no good if I tell her I'm sorry for what I did if we both know I'm really planning to do it again tomorrow. There is no hiding the truth of our hearts from the Lord. He knows our thoughts and our hearts even better than we do. If it's an area you're struggling with, invite Him in to help you. He will do just that! Turning away from that sin or behavior may not be an overnight thing. Sometimes it is, sometimes it is not. But if in your heart you turn from it and invite the Lord to help you, you will notice things begin to change. Know that the Lord always deals with the root causes of our issues. For example, if I am having a hard time quitting alcohol but I repent and ask the Lord to help me, He will help. Sometimes that that results in immediate freedom from drinking but sometimes it is a daily walk as He deals with the root cause of the excessive drinking. However, if I don't confess it and if I am not honest with the Lord about it, sin consciousness will have me slowly turning away from the true source of help.

Sin consciousness will have you thinking that you shouldn't pray, that God is mad at you, or that even though you need His help, you're too unworthy to ask for it. And those thoughts could not be further from the truth! Jesus is our Savior for a reason. We all need salvation, to be saved, rescued. We all need His help.

"Disobedience is like water, it will find every crack and crevice it can expand into. And even though we let water in one way, it never limits itself to that one area of your life. It spills over into almost everything."

A friend of mine was living with her boyfriend and knew that was not God's will for her. She confided in me that every time she was intimate with her boyfriend, she was totally convicted that she was not living the life God desired for her. As a result, she began struggling in her prayer life because she felt conviction and mistook it for the Lord being upset with her and that she wasn't worthy to come before Him in prayer.

I told her instead of running from God, run to Him with that issue. Bring it before Him, talk to Him about it, ask Him to help. He is an ever-present help in the time of trouble! And once she did that, she came back and said, "Angela, I did what you said, and I can hear His voice again!" And it's through her relationship with God through prayer and obedience that she indeed got out of disobedience and all the drama it was causing elsewhere in her life. And be sure, disobedience is like water. It will find every crack and crevice it can expand into. And even though we let that water in one way, it never limits itself to that one area of your life. It spills over into almost everything. Don't let sin consciousness rob you of your time in prayer.

2) Disobedience reduces the effectiveness of communication between you and God.

Hebrews 3:7-10 NET tells us, "So then, as the Holy Spirit says, If you hear God's voice today, do not be stubborn, as your ancestors were when they rebelled against God, as they were that day in the desert when they put him to the test. There they put me to the test and tried me, says God, although they had seen what I did for forty years. And so I was angry with those people and said, 'They are always disloyal and refuse to obey my commands.'"

When we clearly hear what the Lord has instructed us to do, whether that be in the written text of the Bible, through an inner conviction in our heart, or through the voice of the Holy Spirit, it is critical not to just hear but to obey. When we do not obey, our hearts become hardened, especially in that area. The saying goes, "A hard head makes for a soft behind," and so does a hard heart.

In Jewish culture, the Hebrew word for obey is "Shema," which translated in English is best captured by the word "Listen!" When we say listen in this context, it's with the intention that the hearer not just hear what it is we said but act accordingly. We might say, "These children just aren't listening!" We don't just mean that they don't physically hear us, although that is a necessary part. We mean that they aren't doing what we told them to do. That's a close interpretation of Shema. When God communicates with you, He expects Shema! He expects obedience. If no action results from hearing the instructions, what good is it to have heard them? Not much.

When my husband and I get the utility bill each month, they have specific instructions on what to pay and where I can make the payments. But if I don't follow the instructions, after a while, it's going to get very hard to walk around the house at night.

The instructions came with the intent that we would follow them. What we may not be aware of is that Jesus taught us that when we hear but don't obey, we actually put a principle into play that begins the process of dulling our hearing.

To go the necessary step further, it's not only no good, but it is flat out dangerous to hear and not obey. Jesus warns us in Matthew 7:26-27 paraphrase that hearing His words and not doing what He says is like building your house on sand. In the biblical context, Jesus was referring to desert sand that you would find in the wilderness area around Israel. These flood areas are called Wadi. In those areas, it doesn't rain for long periods of time, so the riverbeds dry up and become used for paths and travel and appear to just be part of the landscape. But when it rains, the water doesn't absorb into the earth quickly which causes sudden floods to develop. And although the sky may be clear blue where you are, those floods that begun miles away, tear through. The only warning is the thunderous roar the water makes as it hurls through the Wadi plains. In seconds, the dry land where you may have been standing becomes a raging river. That's a Wadi flood.

If you search on YouTube for sudden Wadi floods, you'll see the numerous examples people have caught on camera. I recommend you take the time to look, it will bring so much clarity to what Jesus taught about when we hear His words and do not obey. As Jesus says, we will be like a man who built his house on desert sand, aka a Wadi, to paraphrase. And when the rains fell, and the floods came, great was the fall of that house. Little to no warning, but complete calamity. This is the metaphor Jesus gives us for hearing but not listening.

The Rewards of Obedience

Our God is a good God! His instructions are always for our good. Following His instructions leads to the following wonderful results.

~ 55:8-11

ur my thoughts are not your thoughts, neither are your ways my ways, declares the Lord. As the heavens are higher than the earth so are my ways higher than your ways and my thoughts than your thoughts. As the heavens are higher than the earth

1 Obedience establishes trust between you and God.

I've come to the realization that when I'm obedient everything will workout for my good. Not necessarily the way I want but because of His Sovereignty, it will be for my good.

Imagine this scenario. We are having a conversation and I say, "Go to the store and when you get there, the store owners are going to give you everything you want for free." Now you have the option to either believe me and go or not believe me and not go. But if you believed me at all, you would make your way to that store and talk to the store owners.

Let's assume you believe me. You get there and you ask for the store owners and they immediately say, "Oh, yes! Angela told us you were coming. Everything you want today is free of charge!" Beyond being excited about what all you may choose to get from the store, what happened to our relationship? Well, I'm willing to go on a limb and say if the next time we talked and I made another promise, you'd be even more inclined to believe me, right? We are developing trust.

The more we obey what the Lord tells us, the more He shows us the benefits of that obedience. And through those experiences, we establish trust in God. We begin to move further and further out into uncharted waters and into things that baffle the "wise." Even in my own story I shared at the beginning of the book, well-meaning people advised me and my husband to separate and divorce. But in my obedience to the Lord's instructions, even when it didn't feel comfortable, even when it didn't look promising, I witnessed the Lord restore our marriage and family to a place better than it was before. My children are happy and thriving. My husband is my best friend and we spend as much time together as we possibly can because we enjoy each other's company so much. That's the reward of obedience and trust. Obedience causes you to win!

2 Obedience allows God's results in your life.

It's easy to get frustrated with prayer when we mix obedience with disobedience, meaning we have half of our heart in doing things our way and half of our heart in doing things God's way. The truth is that we will not get God's results using our ways. If we want God's results in our lives like miracles, healing, deliverance, freedom, and joy, then following His instructions is a pre-requisite. Think about getting an antibiotic from the doctor for an infection but not taking it as directed on the bottle. It may say, "Take two times a day for five days." If you take it every now and then, or only when you feel a symptom of the infection, those antibiotics likely won't do you much good. We need to take God's word and His instructions spoken to our hearts just as prescribed.

3 Obedience will drive out that which is damaging to your life.

The good news about obedience is that it is a separator. Obedience moves you into the plans God has for you and out of the plans the enemy has. As you walk in obedience, harmful things in your life, even if you enjoy them now, will begin leaving your life. Relationships will change, behaviors will change, you will change. Your life will become more and more like God. His favor, His presence, His peace, and His joy will drive out fear, doubt, and confusion that may be present in your life today. It is a process, and the process begins with believing (trusting in, relying on, and obeying).

4 Obedience will drive in that which will cause you to succeed.

Obedience should be done out of love

Obedience is also a magnet. It draws you to purpose and purpose to you. When I became obedient to God's direction to restore my marriage, not only did God do a work in both me and my husband concerning our relationship, but He began to restore me on the inside. That obedience not only impacted my marital relationship, but it impacted every other area of my life as well.

I found that my career got back on track. In my disobedience I had lost direction in my career as well and changed jobs to work for another company that I thought would be better. It wasn't. Within the first three months, I knew I didn't belong there. And though my new employer had given me the title I wanted, I was miserable. The people were distant, and I didn't fit in at all. But as I began to obey the Lord in my marriage, He began working behind the scenes to fix my career as well! God reconnected me to a great colleague from a prior working relationship. Through that reconnection, I was given the opportunity to work at a God-fearing corporation doing the work that I love at a company I love, with people I love working with! And the key, the magnet, was obedience to God. That obedience in the area of my marriage opened doors of success in every other area of my life. The same will happen for you.

"Having an effective prayer life has more to do with the time you spend on your feet than the time you spend on your knees."

" 17 And whatever you do [no matter what it is]
in word or deed, do everything in the name of the
Lord Jesus and in [dependence upon] His Person,
giving praise to God the Father through Him."
COLOSSIAN 3:17 AMPC

5

In The Name.

Have you ever wondered why we end our prayers "in the name of Jesus?" I have, especially at the beginning of my Christian walk. Being an engineer by trade, I was and still am very logic-oriented and rule-based. I wanted to know what the rules were to pray right. I tried with all the logic I could manage to figure out the what, when, and why of praying to God the Father in the name of Jesus. Who did I pray to, Jesus or the Father—or both? And how do you factor in the Holy Spirit? I didn't understand but I knew it was important that I find out.

So what exactly does praying in a name mean anyway? Well, let's dig into that and see what's in a name.

What's In a Name?

GENESIS 17:1-6 NET
When Abram was 99 years old, the Lord appeared to him and said, "I am the sovereign God. Walk before me and be blameless. 2 Then I will confirm my covenant between me and you, and I will give you a multitude of descendants."

3 Abram bowed down with his face to the ground, and God said to him, 4 "As for me, this is my covenant with you: You will be the father of a multitude of nations. 5 No longer will your name be Abram. Instead, your name will be Abraham because I will make you the father of a multitude of nations. 6 I will make you extremely fruitful. I will make nations of you, and kings will descend from you.

Shakespeare posed the question, "What's in a name?" stating that a rose by any other name would smell as sweet. But God has quite a different perspective on that. A name houses four pieces of information about a person. A name holds a person's character, their reputation, their position, and their authority. A name can be so much more than a fancy arrangement of letters; it's who you are.

In fact, in biblical times, names articulated essential characteristics of the person being named. In his article "Naming a Baby," Rabbi Shraga Simmons talks about how Adam considered the characteristics of each animal before giving them a name. He uses the example of a donkey. On English, the word donkey does little to describe the animal, but in Hebrew, the animal is named chamor, from the same root as chomer, which means materialism, and it reflects the key characteristics of an animal known for carrying heavy, physical burdens.

There are more examples in the Bible as well. In Samuel 1, a woman named Hannah is unable to have children and is praying to God intently for a son. The Lord blesses her with what she has asked for and names her son Samuel, which means "God has heard." Again, in Genesis 17:1-6, God appears to Abram when he is ninety-nine years old. God promises him that Abram will have more descendants than there are stars in the sky. But with this promise to Abram, which means "exalted father," God also gives him a new name. A name that will remind him of this promise every time his name is spoken. God names him Abraham, which means "Father of many nations."

Sometimes a name can convey a negative characteristic, as in the case of Jacob. In Genesis 32:28, Jacob had swindled Esau, his brother, out of his birthright as the eldest son. As a result, Esau had become enraged with anger against Jacob and had sworn revenge. Jacob had run away to another land when he received word that Esau and an army of four hundred men were coming his way. That night, as Jacob prepared to meet his brother with gifts to appease him, Jacob found himself wrestling with one of the angels of God demanding a blessing, presumably that he be spared from his brother, Esau. These two wrestle all night and finally, at daybreak, the angel declares to Jacob that he had won. In that moment, the angel gave Jacob a new name.

The name Jacob, which means supplanter, one who takes the place of (another) through force, scheming, and strategy, was exactly the character Jacob had lived up to. As Jacob was seeking to restore his relationship with Esau and pleading for God's mercy, God renamed him Israel. Israel, which means to contend with God, was given because Jacob contended with God's angel and won. Further, it is the name both ancient and modern states of Israel take to this day.

GENESIS 32:28 NKJV
28 And He said, "Your name shall no longer be called Jacob, but Israel; for you have struggled with God and with men, and have prevailed."

Not to beat a dead horse, but there is one more example I would like to give on just how important names are to God. Let's look at Genesis 5 and the lineage of Adam through Noah. As we go through each name, we note of the meaning of each name.

Adam – **Man**

Seth – **Appointed**

Enosh – **Mortal**

Kanan – **Lamenter/Sorrow**

Mahalelalel – **Praise of God**

Jared – **shall come down**

Enoch – **Mouth/Trained/Teaching**

Methuselah – **When He Is Dead It Shall Be Sent**

Lamech – **the low/depressed/despair**

Noah – **rest**

If we put that into a sentence, it reads,
"Man appointed mortal sorrow, the praise of God shall come down teaching when He is Dead it shall be sent, the despairing rest."

My common English version of that reflects that one man appointed to all men sorrow, but the praise of God (e.g., Jesus) shall come down teaching that when He is crucified, the despairing shall be sent rest."

In other words, the very basis of the Gospel. There are other ways to translate each name resulting in different sentence, but I find it fascinating how intentional God is.

In addition to a name revealing character, a name also conveys a person's reputation. When we think about Jesus, we know he had a reputation of always being obedient to God the Father, even to the point of death. He also had a reputation for every one of His prayers being answered, and believe you me, the two are directly related.

A name conveys position and authority, even in the common workplace. If I worked at Microsoft, for example, and I heard, "Hey Angela, Bill Gates is coming to visit you today," his name would invoke a certain response because he was the principal founder of Microsoft. If during that visit Bill said, "Angela, tell the team I want them to all take the afternoon off." I would go out and say, "Hey, team! Bill Gates said he wants each of us to take the rest of the day off!" Would they take off? Of course! Because I effectively said, "In the name of Bill Gates, on his behalf I am speaking and with the authority that his position brings, take the afternoon off." All of that is encompassed in a name.

And guess what? Jesus Christ, son of the living God, who has the name that is above all names, has said, use His name! When the scripture tells us to use the name of Jesus, it's telling us to use His reputation, established by His character, supported by His position as son of God, King of Kings, and Lord of Lords, and enforced by His God-given authority. Now that's a name! We see this over and over again in Scripture:

"And when that time comes, you will ask nothing of Me [you will need to ask Me no questions]. I assure you, most solemnly I tell you, that My Father will grant you whatever you ask in My Name [as presenting all that I Am]. Up to this time you have not asked a [single] thing in My Name [as presenting all that I Am]; but now ask and keep on asking and you will receive, so that your joy (gladness, delight) may be full and complete."

JOHN 16:22-24 AMPC

"And such some of you were [once]. But you were washed clean (purified by a complete atonement for sin and made free from the guilt of sin), and you were consecrated (set apart, hallowed), and you were justified [pronounced righteous, by trusting] in the name of the Lord Jesus Christ and in the [Holy] Spirit of our God."

1 CORINTHIANS 6:11 AMP

"And these attesting signs will accompany those who believe: in My name they will drive out demons; they will speak in new languages; They will pick up serpents; and [even] if they drink anything deadly, it will not hurt them; they will lay their hands on the sick, and they will get well."

MARK 16:17-18

What's key in each of these scriptures and more is "in the name!" In the character, in the reputation, in the position, and in the authority of Jesus Christ. Jesus said, "Ask the Father, in My name, and He will grant you whatever you ask." That's why it's so important to know what "in His name" means.

MATTHEW 1:21 AMP
"She will give birth to a Son, and you shall name Him Jesus (The Lord is salvation), for He will save His people from their sins."

Praying in the Name

When we pray to the Father in the name of Jesus, we are covering a lot of ground. It's so much more than a formal religious closing. I'm telling you now, if you were to use my name it wouldn't get you very far. I can imagine the Father now saying, "Did you just say in Angela's name, amen? I'm looking at her character, position, authority, and reputation, and uh.... she needs a Savior herself!"

There's only one name given to us by which we can be saved. And His name itself means Salvation!

Matthew 1:21 AMP, "She will give birth to a Son, and you shall name Him Jesus (The Lord is salvation), for He will save His people from their sins."

When we pray in the name of Jesus, we admit that our own name just won't do. We are saying our personal names are bankrupt. We are spiritually filing chapter 11. We owe debts we cannot pay, nor do we qualify for leniency. But through our union with Jesus, we are like a bride who takes on her husband's name—and the husband is willing and able to pay every debt we ever incurred. Not to mention His credit score is perfect!

"The power of God is in the character of God. And His character is represented in His name."

When we pray in the name of Jesus, we pray in His authority. I like how Rick Ezell uses the analogy of a child putting on a policeman's uniform and directing traffic. The cars adhere to the child's direction, not because of the child, but because of the authority that uniform represents. And if the child has acquired that uniform, they must have acquired the authority that goes along with it. In the name of Jesus, we clothe ourselves in Christ!

As long as the child directs traffic in alignment with the will of the police officer, drivers adhere. But if the child should begin directing in a way that creates chaos, drivers will quickly begin to challenge that authority and stop obeying. If we pray in alignment with the will of Jesus as revealed by His word, we too can direct traffic.

When we pray in the name of Jesus, we are representing His interests here on earth. Much like a legal power of attorney where one person may represent another in his absence and act in their behalf, Jesus has given every believer unlimited and general power of attorney in every matter and with the right to use his name in every situation.

As a result, we begin every prayer or end every prayer in the name of Jesus. Or better yet, let's do like Colossians 3:17 AMP instructs: *"And whatever you do [no matter what it is] in word or deed, do everything in the name of the Lord Jesus and in [dependence upon] His Person, giving praise to God the Father through Him."*

"On your feet now—applaud God!
Bring a gift of laughter,
sing yourselves into his presence.
Know this: God is God, and God, God.
He made us; we didn't make Him.
We're his people, his well-tended sheep.
Enter with the password: 'Thank you!'
Make yourselves at home, talking praise.
Thank him. Worship him.
For God is sheer beauty, all-generous in
love, loyal always and ever."

PSALMS 100:1-5 MSG

6 Use the Password

Just as I begin most of my prayers with, "Father, in the name of Jesus..." I also begin with simply saying thank You. Why? Because just like that scripture says, it's like a password! It opens the door to our hearts and engages us with Him. It positions us to experience God. In other words, it's a key.

A perfect example of how Jesus responds to a thankful heart is found in Mark 10. Let me summarize the story. Jesus, on His way to Jerusalem, had to pass through Samaria and Galilee. On the way, he came across ten lepers in need of His help. They cried, saying, "Jesus, Master, have mercy on us!" And when Jesus saw them, He told them exactly what to do. He said, "Go and show yourselves to the priests." And as they went, they were healed from leprosy!

MARK 10:51-52 KJV

51 And Jesus answered and said unto him, What wilt thou that I should do unto thee? The blind man said unto him, Lord, that I might receive my sight. 52 And Jesus said unto him, Go thy way; thy faith hath made thee whole. And immediately he received his sight, and followed Jesus in the way.

Now, here's where it gets even more interesting. When one of the ten lepers saw that he was healed, he turned back around and went to Jesus. With a heart full of gratitude, he fell down at Jesus's feet and gave him thanks. In other words, it wasn't merely lip service, he acted upon his gratitude by actually going back to see Jesus face to face. His actions showed how thankful he was. So Jesus said to this man, "Weren't there ten of you healed? Where are the other nine?"

The Bible doesn't say any more about those other nine, but it does say what happened to the one who was thankful. It says that for the man who came back, Jesus said, "Go your way, your faith has made you whole"(paraphrase Mark 10:46-52)

Not just healed, whole! His heart of thankfulness put that Samaritan man in position for even more! He not only received the healing he asked for, but he received the wholeness he needed. Now, there's a big difference between being healed and being whole. Leprosy is a disease that causes pale or pinkish patches to occur on the skin. Over time, those areas become insensitive to temperature or pain. It causes nerve problems and infections, can result in tissue loss, or can cause fingers and toes to become shortened and deformed as cartilage is absorbed into the body. To be healed of this disease is to no longer have it active in the body, but the damage caused by the disease remains. To be made whole, however, is to completely restore the body back to its original state; just as if the disease never happened.

It's the difference between the Lord healing a marriage, keeping it together, and Him making the marriage whole, removing the past hurts and emotional baggage — as if the tearing apart never happened. It's the difference between Jesus healing me from depression and suicidal thoughts and Him making me whole such that I radiate with joy and life as if I never suffered from that a day in my life. Healing addresses our future, wholeness eradicates our past.

We want to be healed and whole, yes?! We start with being thankful. Proverbs says, "Out of the abundance of the heart, the mouth speaks." When we are genuinely thankful, it will spill over into words and it will display in what we do. It's through a heart of thanksgiving that we position ourselves for the power of God to flow in our lives and circumstances.

If you can, think about a time when someone did something big for you. If you were thankful, how did you show that you were? How much more should we show God how appreciative we are of His love and salvation?

> *"Don't worry about anything; instead,*
> *pray about everything. Tell God what you need and thank*
> *him for all he has done."*
> **PHILIPPIANS 4:6 NLT**

Now that we've covered what being thankful is and how it opens doors for us, let's talk about the other side of gratitude. When we are not grateful, we are ungrateful.

"Healing addresses our future, wholeness eradicates our past."

That's kind of like a "duh, Angela" statement but really, nobody walks around saying, "I'm not grateful at all for anything, ever." At least, I sure hope not. In the same way that truly being thankful shows up in our worship and our words, being ungrateful shows in our complaining. Although we may not say we aren't thankful, we sure can complain.

I used to be complain-chief, until I heard this powerful statement on complaining. During Sunday Service a few years ago, my pastor/husband said, "You know what complaining really is? When you complain, you are effectively telling God that you think He is incompetent."

Whoa, say what now? I thought. I'm telling the Almighty that I have something to say about His performance as God? Oh boy, that can't be good. I immediately repented and asked for His mercy. The pastor continued to minister but I had to take a few minutes to pray and tell the Lord I was sorry. He's my friend and I never want to insult my friend, much less the Most High God.

When we complain about where we are or what situation we're in, when we complain about all that doesn't seem quite the way we would like it to be in our lives, we are effectively saying, "Creator God... the One Who formed the universe without any of my help at all, I think You're messing up. You didn't need the counsel of any man to create this earth, but in my limited thinking, I've formed an opinion that You don't know what You're doing. Little ol' me thinks that great big You are incompetent."

Of course, there are situations and circumstances that we are not fond of. I'm not talking about that. I'm talking about the times where those thoughts run through our minds and we set ourselves in agreement with them. The best Biblical example we have of this is the children of Israel when they were delivered from Egypt and found themselves wandering through the desert.

They had just been delivered from years of slavery and ungodly hard labor, every day. The Lord heard their cry and sent multiple plagues to Egypt to soften the heart of Pharaoh so that he would set the Israelites free. And Pharaoh did just that. As they travelled to a new land, God provided them with bread from heaven (manna) to feed and sustain them along the way.

"The rabble among them [who followed Israel from Egypt] had greedy desires [for familiar and delicious food], and the Israelites wept again and said, 'Who will give us meat to eat? We remember the fish we ate freely and without cost in Egypt, the cucumbers, melons, leeks, onions, and garlic. But now our appetite is gone; there is nothing at all [in the way of food] to be seen but this manna.'"
NUMBERS 11:4-6 AMP

Instead of continuing to be thankful for their freedom, they decided to complain about the circumstances of their journey. The story is very interesting, and I encourage you to read how the Lord dealt with their complaints. It may be where we get the phrase, "Be careful what you pray for, you just might get it."

Suffice it to say that their complaining didn't sit well with God—at all. He sent quail to their camp. So much quail that they ate and ate and ate. That place was called the "Grave of gluttony" because all those who complained and ate the quail died of a sickness the quail brought, Thank God for Jesus! Through Jesus, today we experience the grace and mercy of God and don't answer for our complaining in the way the Israelites did, but we certainly nullify our effectiveness in prayer. If thankfulness is the password that opens the door to the throne of God in prayer, complaining closes the door and locks it shut. You may as well put up a sign that says, "Do Not Enter."

Even now, I ask that the Holy Spirit show us every area in our lives where we find ourselves complaining and lead us to a place of repentance in that area. Let's do what the children of Israel so often did not: see that God is always working on our behalf. Therefore, in faith we say, "Lord, I'm so very thankful today because I know, according to Your Word, which You always perform, that all things are working together for my good because I love You and I am called by You. For it is written in Your Word: 'And we know [with great confidence] that God [who is deeply concerned about us] causes all things to work together [as a plan] for good for those who love God, to those who are called according to His plan and purpose'(Romans 8:28 AMP). Thank You Lord, I qualify for this promise!"

ROMANS 8:28 AMP
"And we know [with great confidence] that God [who is deeply concerned about us] causes all things to work together [as a plan] for good for those who love God, to those who are called according to His plan and purpose.

"But we are not of those who shrink back
and are destroyed, but of those who
believe and are saved.
HEBREWS 10:39

7 Believe!

Now is a good time to take a moment and ask, do you really believe prayer works?

I believe the company I work for will deposit my agreed upon salary into my bank account on time every two weeks. I believe it so much that I spend at least eight hours a day, five days a week working for them. In fact, when I first started working there, I showed up for two whole weeks before getting paid a dime.

When I got serious about losing weight (one of many, many times), I got up early in the morning, went to the gym to exercise, and followed a sound eating plan. Did I always want to? Ha, I promise you I did not. So why did I put in that time and effort? Because I believed my trainer and that if I did as I was told, my body would respond and let go of some unwanted weight. In both cases, I believed, and therefore I spent time doing.

Here's my point: What you believe, you'll do. When you believe prayer works, you will spend time doing it. That's not to say you won't face opposition, distractions, and the busyness of life. I guarantee that you will. But when you truly believe in the power of prayer, you won't let anything stop you.

Just Enough To Try

"And this is the confidence (the assurance, the privilege of boldness) which we have in Him: [we are sure] that if we ask anything (make any request) according to His will (in agreement with His own plan), He listens to and hears us."

1 JOHN 5:14 AMPC

How do you become confident in anything? Through experience. In Romans 8:38, Paul writes that he was not only confident, but he was fully persuaded! Fully persuaded that nothing can separate us from the love of God which is in Jesus. How did he become persuaded? Through experience.

Experience with God comes from time spent with God and there is simply no substitute for it. When we take God at His word and believe, we give Him the opportunity to prove Himself in our lives. Jesus told each of the disciples to follow Him. They believed Him enough to put down their own businesses, jobs, everything and follow. As they followed they developed a relationship with Jesus. They saw Him perform many miracles, they studied at His feet and learned from Him, they walked with Him every day. Through their experiences with Him they came to know Him not only as Jesus, but as Messiah.

When I began my walk with Jesus, I was so excited about my new life that I tried to mature into a twenty-year veteran within two months' time. It didn't work. Like a baby without teeth trying to eat meat, I spiritually choked. I found myself spitting out what I couldn't chew. I tried my best to catch the truths of what was being taught but a lot of what was being said was way over my head. Yet the more I heard, the more I understood. It took time and experience because experience comes over time. The life of a Christian believer isn't a race, it's a marathon. Take your time, sit in it. Set yourself to engage on the journey for the long haul.

The more you practice believing, the more you will experience God. It's like developing a muscle. My daughters and I started an obstacle course training class. We love watching the show "American Ninja Warrior" so we decided to give obstacle training a try. On my first day, we worked on monkey bars. They expected me to go across

The life of a Christian believer is not a race, it's a marathon. Take your time, sit in it. Set yourself to engage on the journey

"Believe just enough to try."

those bars like the kids were. (Yes, I'm in the kiddie class but that's another story).

I watched all the kids fly across the bars and I stood there thinking about how my upper body strength clearly has not kept up with my lower body weight over the years. I was certain I wasn't going to be able to do it. And I was right; didn't even make it to the second bar. So, I began working on my upper body strength at home by doing assisted pull ups — assisted pull ups being one of the skills we must demonstrate to progress to the next rank. Not being one to take my time moving through levels, ranking up became my driving motivation. That night I found the nearest thing to a pull up bar I could find in my house which was on my treadmill. I grabbed the bar, stretched out my feet, and began trying to pull myself up to the bar. My goal was to do ten but I was struggling after the first three. My daughter, being naturally athletic, cheered me on.

When I finally finished, she looked at me with both sympathy and caution in her eyes and said, "Well Mommy, about the next rank, it's gonna be awhile." She was being sincere, but I cracked up laughing. She was right! I had a very long way to go before I would be moving on to the next level.

Fast forward two months. We were going to class twice a week, working on pull ups at home, but despite my good intentions, I had yet to drop a pound. But guess who was flying through six monkey bars? Okay, flying might be a bit of an exaggeration but yes, me! I went from barely being able to hold myself on the pull up bar to being able to do a full scale, non-assisted pull up even! It took time, practice, and experience, but I did it. My muscles got stronger every day and I was able to make great progress. I followed the instructions and I watched other people do it well.

It's the same way with believing! The more you do it, the stronger and better you get at it. I began my pull up progress with a first step of faith and following the instructions. I believed just enough to try. I listened to the instructor, understood what he said to do, and I tried it. I didn't do it right the first time, but I didn't quit. I simply tried again. The instructor was right there to assist me and keep me from hurting myself. And that's just what I'm encouraging you to do in prayer. With Jesus as your instructor, believe just enough to try. I mean letting go of the bar to reach out and grab the next bar, knowing there is a real possibility you could fall, and still trying. These are the moments with God that build your foundation. These are the experiences that lead you to a place of being fully persuaded.

This is believing and our starting point in prayer. ⚬⚯

How we spend our days, is, of course, how
we spend our lives.
- ANNIE DILLARD

8 It's About Time.

Prayer is an essential part of your relationship with God. But there is no relationship without fellowship. I can't say I'm a good mom if I never spend time with my girls talking and just hanging out with them. Sure, I provide their food, shelter, and clothing, get them to school, and help with homework. I even spend time taking them to their extra-curricular activities, like dance and basketball. But they don't need me to just do for them.

They need me to talk to them, to listen, to play, to be available. It's in those moments we develop our relationship. In the times of fellowship, conversation, laughing, crying, playing, correcting, and simply just being there, we form bonds that will last forever.

The more time we spend together, the more we get to know each other. In prayer, we spend time sharing our hearts with God and we spend time listening to His. In the time with God, we read the Bible (His word), asking the Holy Spirit to show and teach us about what we are reading. Prayer is recognizing His presence with you as you go about your everyday life. It's thanking Him for being with you everywhere you go. Prayer is calling out to God for help in times when things don't go the way we want them to. Prayer is developed in life, and living life takes time. Prayer is more than the words you speak, it's also in the life you live.

When I first began to pray with a dependence on the Lord to cause a change to occur and not just praying like it's a good backup plan in case my efforts failed, I saw a complete difference in the results I was having. When I reached that point, I had already tried everything I knew to do, and not only did I fail, but my actions were making things even worse. Maybe I'm the only one guilty of this, but I used to approach prayer like, "OK, I've tried everything else, I've got nothing else to lose, may as well see if God can do anything with this." Looking back, that was awful! I was like this story of a child and his father scaling up a mountain. After trying and trying until he was worn out, the child finally said, "Daddy, I give up, will you carry me?" The father looks at the child and sees he's only made it 5 ft. up a 1000-ft. climb. So he picks the child up and carries him in his child carrying backpack and scales the mountain with ease. When they reach the top, the father turns to his son and says, "This was my plan all along." Ever since I realized how much better life was, how much more effective my prayers are than my trying on my own, I have begun praying first and doing second. That habit takes practice. Prayer takes practice. The more time I spend praying and obeying, the better I become at both. The more time I spend in prayer, the more comfortable I get doing it.

Make Time

The Lord will never force you to pray. He will nudge you, encourage you, and prompt you, but never force. Unfortunately, that means if you don't make time to do it, it won't be done. Period. If we must restructure morning routines to make time for it, let's restructure. People have varying schedules and routines but beginning the day (whenever that is for you) with time in meditation and prayer is the best way to start the day.

I use the word meditation to convey the idea of getting control over your thoughts and bringing yourself to a place of internal quietness. Reading the Bible is a great approach. I begin most of my morning prayers in meditation.

If you're anything like me, when you begin to pray, your mind starts racing. All kinds of thoughts start surfacing, reminding you of what all you have to do, reminding you of problems you have, anything and everything it seems like. I've heard some people say they bring a notepad and write down all those reminders, so they can move past it. Matter of fact, I highly recommend making a habit of bringing a Bible, a pen, and a notebook with you in prayer, expecting to receiving instructions. Invite and welcome the Holy Spirit in to help you pray. Then begin praying in the name of Jesus with thanksgiving and go from there.

As you pray, spend time in meaningful silence. Meaningful silence is time we spend intentionally listening to hear the Holy Spirit. It's not listening with your head and the thoughts running through your mind, it's listening with your belly. It sounds like an odd place but that is where your spiritual ears are. You hear people say, "Listen to your gut." That's where the Holy Spirit speaks. You may not always hear Him speak during prayer, but when you do, write down what He says. No matter how big or how small, make a note of it. You cannot do what you don't remember. There are so many lost moments I have because I just knew I would remember what He told me and then two days later I forgot. Please learn from my misstep there and write it down. If it wasn't important, He wouldn't bother telling you.

The more time you spend praying and obeying, the stronger your relationship will be. The stronger the relationship, the deeper the communication.

Reverence The Time

"The fear of the Lord is the beginning of wisdom, And the knowledge of the Holy One is understanding."

PROVERBS 9:10

PROVERBS 9:10 MSG
Skilled living gets its start in the Fear-of-God, insight into life from knowing a Holy God.

The word fear here is not the scary fear, it's a fear that reflects the idea of living in respect, awe, and submission. This idea of respect is reflected in how we pray as well. There are times when I simply sit up in my bed and pray, but rarely do I experience God in as deep a way as when I go to my regular meeting spot and kneel before Him. It's my way of saying, "Lord, I'm more concerned about talking with You than I am with being comfortable."

I've made a space in my bedroom closet for my time in prayer. In this space, I have my prayer board where I write down testimonies of what God has done for me. I have a notepad and a pen so that I am prepared to write as I'm led by the Holy Spirit. I also have a pillow so that my back doesn't hurt while I'm kneeling. I even have a blanket because I don't like being cold. Pain and cold can be distractions to me in prayer. I keep my Tallit (prayer shawl) there as well. It's my own private, personal space. It's my dedicated space where God and I fellowship in the mornings. I added those things to my prayer space over time out of reverence and respect—the fear of the Lord. And the result I get is just as Proverbs 9:10 says, "skilled living," and for me it starts right there. The more serious I become about prayer, the more seriously I treat my time praying.

"Knowing trees, I understand the
meaning of patience. Knowing grass, I can
appreciate persistence."
-HAL BORLAND

Persistence

PERSISTENCE [per-sis-tuh ns, -zis-] derived from the root word persist, a verb meaning:

01. to continue steadfastly or firmly in some state, purpose, course of action, or the like, especially in spite of opposition, remonstrance, etc.:

02. to last or endure tenaciously:

03. to be insistent in a statement, request, question, etc.

Persistence is not my favorite word, nor does it come to me naturally. We live in a culture today that seems to oppose the very concept of persisting. In fact, it almost trains it out of you. We don't like to wait for anything. Our lives have become so busy that cooking a frozen meal in the microwaves for five minutes seems unnecessarily long. In fact, our food industry is so speed oriented that Mc-Donald's is working on a lane system that they predict will shorten the line wait time down to ninety seconds. Why that's even a need speaks to our desire to hurry and their desire to hurry us. As a culture, we want what we want, and we want it right now.

It took me five years to put on an extra twenty lbs. but when my trainer said it would take at least four months to drop it, I thought about getting a new trainer! I want to be fit right here, right now.

And most of us do the very same with God. We want our prayers answered right here, right now. We may have spent years making bad decisions about our finances but expect God to bail us out of our financial ditch with one month of prayer and no real sacrifice or change on our end. I've seen people stop attending church after three months, saying God doesn't work for them. I want to ask, "Didn't it take you thirty years to make this mess? God is doing the best He can with what you gave Him to work with." Some situations take sheer persistence in prayer. Jesus gave this parable:

> *Jesus told them a story showing that it was neces-*
> *sary for them to pray consistently and never quit.*
> *He said, "There was once a judge in some city who*
> *never gave God a thought and cared nothing for*
> *people. A widow in that city kept after him: 'My*
> *rights are being violated. Protect me!'*

"He never gave her the time of day. But after this went on and on he said to himself, 'I care nothing what God thinks, even less what people think. But because this widow won't quit badgering me, I'd better do something and see that she gets justice—otherwise I'm going to end up beaten black-and-blue by her pounding.'"

Then the Master said, "Do you hear what that judge, corrupt as he is, is saying? So what makes you think God won't step in and work justice for his chosen people, who continue to cry out for help? Won't he stick up for them? I assure you, he will. He will not drag his feet. But how much of that kind of persistent faith will the Son of Man find on the earth when he returns?" **LUKE 18:1-8 MSG**

Relationships take persistence in prayer, and family can take even more. Raising children takes persistence in prayer. Finding and fulfilling your purpose in life takes persistence in prayer. Success takes persistence in prayer. Daily persistent prayer is like a compass rose. You begin by heading in a general direction, say North, but the more you pray and fellowship with the Lord, the more precise your needle becomes. Your directions transform from just North to North-Northwest. The closer you get, the more precise the heading. Over time and as you cover more ground, the directions become the exact degrees you need to get you to your destination.

"Prayer takes persistence, but He gives us the strength to persist."

When I started this writing journey, the Lord gave me a general heading. He said, "Write!" He pointed me North. And as I spent time in persistent prayer, He narrowed down the topic, North-Northwest.

As I began writing, He gave me the degrees. Yet even though I know this pattern and principle in God, it can be hard to do some days. I have my own thoughts, emotions, and ways of being that He is correcting in me. There were times when my husband and I were reconciling and establishing our new normal that I was tempted to still give up. It seemed too hard and that God was moving too slow. I did mention patience wasn't my strongest attribute, yes? But as I chose to persist anyway, I continued to see Him restore our marriage.

There were other times, like in writing this book even, that doubt surfaced, and I was afraid of failing. Who am I to be writing a book on prayer? I thought. But as I acknowledged those thoughts and fears in prayer, the Lord gave me the courage and fortitude I needed to persist. Even in persisting, He helps us to persist! When life got very busy, working long hours and raising two kids and supporting my husband as a pastor's wife, I didn't know how to make time to write. But every encouraging word I needed was there. Every support I needed, He made sure I had. Prayer takes persistence, but He gives us the strength to persist.

One of the women on our church's intercessory prayer team is a nurse in the Neonatal Intensive Care Unit (NICU). Recently, there was a young lady who had a baby girl at twenty-five weeks gestation. The baby was struggling to survive, as you can imagine. She weighed 1 pound 12 ounces and was on 100 percent oxygen. The doctors told the mom they had done all they could do for her and had little to no expectation for the baby to make it. Having been in a similar, but not as dire, situation as this mom, I knew she must have been feeling powerless and helpless as she stayed by her baby's side every moment, praying for her life.

Our prayer team member, the nurse, saw what was going on and just felt an incredible need to pray with the mom for her baby. She called my husband, her pastor, to pray and hear from God as well. When she wasn't able to reach him, she left him a text message about the situation. So he prayed and sent her a text back with what the Lord laid on his heart to do.

The nurse didn't get the text message until the close of her shift. She had scrubbed out and taken off her sanitized clothes and was heading home. But when she read the text message, she knew it was important and turned back around, scrubbed back in, clothed back up, and went back into the room where the baby was. The other nurses said, "I thought you were gone for the night." She replied that she was but had some unfinished business. Right there in the middle of the room, she prayed for the baby girl as the Lord had instructed. Then she turned around to go home. Before she could leave, the baby's need for oxygen decreased to 75 percent and had an immediate turnaround.

When she told us what happened we were elated and knew the Lord was working on the mom's behalf. Even the doctors were amazed at this, the baby had officially turned a corner none had predicted she would turn.

The baby has continued to improve but the mom's journey isn't over. The baby was sent to another, better equipped facility at the mom's request where she can get the best care. This is where her persistence in prayer must come in.

Undoubtedly there are many obstacles and hurdles she will face as the baby continues to grow, and it's through persistence, not giving up regardless of what the doctors' reports say, refusing to quit or back down on her faith, through her time spent in prayer, getting her precise compass rose headings that we fully expect to see her baby thrive. And I pray the Lord continues to give her everything she needs to persist.

I'm sure you have your own story and need for persistence in prayer. Whatever your situation or need you may have, persist! Refuse to give up.

"16 And I will ask the Father, and He will give you another Comforter (Counselor, Helper, Intercessor, Advocate, Strengthener, and Standby), that He may remain with you forever. 17 The Spirit of Truth, Whom the world cannot receive (welcome, take to its heart), because it does not see Him or know and recognize Him. But you know and recognize Him, for He lives with you [constantly] and will be in you."

JOHN 14:16-17 AMPC

10

Partnering with the Holy Spirit

The Holy Spirit is the Spirit of God. God is expressed in three persons, so united in purpose they are one. The Father, the Son, and the Holy Spirit. Each unique yet the same. There is so much to learn and to teach about the Holy Spirit that I won't try to do that here in this one chapter. The personality and character of the Holy Spirit that is essential for this chapter, however, is the one of being our Teacher.

It's the Holy Spirit who teaches us to pray, it is the Holy Spirit who even reveals to us what we need to pray for. It is the Holy Spirit who knows the mind of God and knows God's plan for you. He knows why you were created, He knows what you are here for, and just as importantly, He knows how to guide you to fulfilling your destiny. And He eagerly desires to share it with you. Here are a few key character traits we need to know about Him, for this chapter:

He is a Person. He's not a feeling, He's not something you "catch." He's not some fast-paced music played in church with people yelling andshouting. The Holy Spirit is not an emotion. There are certainly times when I sense His presence and I am emotionally moved, but the emotions are just a by-product.

He is a Gentleman. He's far too precious to be intrusive. If you don't open your heart to Him, if you don't take the time to learn to hear him, He will simply wait until you do.

He is Truth. *Let me restate that as a fact:* The Holy Spirit is the Truth. He is never wrong. Like never ever wrong. That's important because as we discuss partnering with the Holy Spirit in prayer, we need to know that what He says and what He reveals is the truth. Sometimes He will tell us things that in our limited mental thinking we immediately try to reason away. Let me warn you, you can convince or reason anything you want, but it will neither make what the Holy Spirit said wrong nor you right.

In my prayer closet, I keep a memo board of people, ideas, dreams, and goals. Many people would call my board a vision board but it's not that. It's my prayer board. The difference is that everything on that board represents an area I am partnering with the Holy Spirit on to see happen. And because I'm partnering with Him, not the other way around, He calls the shots. Everything that goes up on that board I pray about to make sure it's what He is leading me to put there. This is part of the process that takes time because I don't always get it right immediately.

A few years ago, I put the names and titles of these road races I wanted to run in. I'm not a runner, never have been. Sometimes I enjoy it, but when I tell you that I am a slow runner, I mean some people may walk faster than I run. My fastest mile to date was still more than thirteen minutes. But I had the notion to get in shape and become a runner. I got pictures of people running and images of the medals they handed out at these races for finishing and put them on my prayer board. I figured (and whenever you or I figure anything, that should be red flag! We want the Holy Spirit to reveal, not us to be "figuring"), yes, I figured that since the Holy Spirit had been impressing on my heart the need to be healthy and active, running was a great way to achieve that. I prayed about me running in those races and reminded myself that "faith without works is dead." And, being a logical-minded engineer, I

> *What I love about the Holy Spirit is that He can take your target and fix your aim.*

COLOSSIANS 3:15 NET
Let the peace of Christ be in control in your heart (for you were in fact called as one body to this peace), and be thankful.

researched the best shoes, the best activity tracking watches, the best apps. And then I began running. First one mile, then two. And guess what? I found it to be boring and my knees hurt and instead of looking forward to that part of the morning, I began to find any reason not to. Those races that led up to a 10 miler came and went and I was still struggling to get through my second mile. My time improved from 14:43 to 13:52. I told you I am a slow runner. And I took those pictures off my board. Why? Because that had all been me and my figuring.

What I love about the Holy Spirit is that He can take your target and fix your aim. So after more time in prayer and listening and being led, I ended up connecting with a personal trainer who lived over 300 miles away. He sent me my workouts for the week, my eating plans for the week, and followed up with me daily. I found a Christian motivational speaker on YouTube who had great music and great words to keep me pumped and I listened to that every workout. Four months later, I was down seventeen pounds and feeling fantastic!

It wasn't that the trainer was so great, it was more about me yielding to the Holy's Spirit's guidance than insisting I figure it out on my own.

With that lesson learned, I went back and updated my board. I prayed and took time to hear from the Holy Spirit on each item or concept I had on my board. I would focus on each thing and if I didn't have that inner peace about it, it came off. Some things I really wanted but no matter how excited or passionate I was about it, if I didn't have peace deep down, I let it go. I remember working for a company that I did not like. The people weren't nice, the people in charge were more arrogant than competent, and I did not fit in at all. But a friend of mine called me and told me about where they were working and the kind of culture they had established, and I knew that's where I belonged. They were doing the kind of work I wanted to be a part of. So, I prayed, and the Lord confirmed it was where I belonged by giving me a knowing peace.

That next morning in prayer, I wrote down the company's name and the salary I wanted and posted it on my prayer board. For months I would read it and be reminded about what the Lord had in store for me and I thanked Him for it. That kept me going during the mornings where I dreaded going to where I was at the time. Then the day came that my friend called and said he had an opportunity that I might be interested in! Long story short, I took the job with exactly the salary I had written on my board. To this day I work there and love it more than any place I've ever worked.

It was in these types of situations and experiences that I really learned how to let the peace of God rule. As Colossians 3:15 says, "And let the peace of God rule in your hearts, to the which also ye are called in one body; and be ye thankful." The more experiences I have like this, partnering with the Holy Spirit, the more familiar I become with that peace. And if I have something I'm praying about that doesn't have that same peace, I know it's not Him and to leave it alone. When we stay

"The enemy and life in general are designed to challenge the authenticity of our walk"

partnered with the Holy Spirit, we experience success.

There are times when that partnership is challenged. The enemy and life in general are designed to challenge the authenticity of our walk with God. Sometimes that challenge, those fights, are often experienced through those closest to us — our family, our friends, our jobs, and even ourselves. Here's an example of what I mean:

Expect to Fight

Running upstairs to my place of prayer, tears streaming down my face, I cried out to God asking Him to help me. Turmoil had just broken out in my home and I felt like I wanted to explode in anger. I hadn't seen the argument coming, it just happened. But it seemed to happen on exactly the wrong day, at precisely the wrong time. Those days that feel like perfect storms are no accident —those are attacks.

Having always been a top performer in school and at work, I considered myself to be a smart woman. I never had a hard time catching onto concepts or coming up with ideas. It had been part of my success. But during this particular season of my life, I found myself struggling to pull my thoughts together. Quite frankly, I was scared. One thing my career required was that I be sharp 24/7. Other people I worked with were top-notch, smart, witty, and great at what they did. Now being at a smaller company, my team was less than twenty people, each hand-picked to work there. They were over-achievers and quick thinkers. It was a wonderful team and I didn't want to be the weakest link, especially being that I was their manager, the fearless leader tasked to herd the cats and lead them to success. Although I was the newest person on the team, I had managed much larger teams of engineers before and knew I was quite capable of doing the job. But for some reason, I was experiencing brain fog like never before. It was like I had ten feet of visibility for a one-mile drive. My words wouldn't flow, my thoughts would fade before I could fully think them through. It was bad, and I was struggling. What's worse is that I was too scared to tell anybody, so I didn't.

I knew my manager believed I was competent, but not having worked with me for that long, he was probably beginning to have doubts. I would have had them too if I were him. I almost botched a meeting with a key customer because my sentences were about as elegant as a five-year-old's. I found enough moments of clarity to do okay, but I knew I wasn't operating at 100 percent. I was maxing myself out at 50 percent and that was by sheer prayer. If I didn't have clarity on anything else, it was the ability to pray, "Holy Spirit, I need Your help!"

So of course, the adversary was right there to keep pushing my buttons. "Remember your Aunt Sara and your Aunt Ariel? Didn't they die with dementia? It's in your DNA."

I knew better than to entertain those thoughts and I certainly was NOT about to agree with it. I was barely forty years old and had way too much life to live and purpose to walk out for that. Nope, not having full brain function was not an option, but it remained the threat lurking in the dark recesses of my mind. No pun intended.

So, there I was internally fighting for my ability to think, trying to learn everything I can about healthy eating, going non-stop all week, every week. Monday through Friday work, do homework and activities with the girls in the evenings, Saturday chore day, and Sundays at church. I rarely got time to be to myself, which as an introvert meant I was drained.

And in the middle of all that — boom! My husband and I had an argument that escalated further than we should have allowed. We realized we were out of order, stopped fighting, and went to our individual corners. He went outside, and I came upstairs to pray.

"Lord Jesus," I cried, "help me!" On my knees, face to the floor sobbing, I was spent, exhausted, and irate. After I calmed down a bit, I sensed the Holy Spirit led me to pray, "What weapon do I use in this fight?" I knew it wasn't my husband I was fighting with. I was fighting my past hurts and my present fear. I was fighting insecurity, I was fighting loneliness, I was fighting my emotions that wanted to lose control. I found depression looking in to see if there was an opportunity. I saw suicide looking from the distance, cheering depression on. All these opposing forces were congratulating each other for the role they had played in orchestrating the storm that they hoped would open the door to their entry back into my life.

"Use the weapon of praise," I sensed the Lord reply. Right there, tears falling and nose running, I began to

2 CORINTHIANS 10:4

AMP *"For the weapons of our warfare are not physical [weapons of flesh and blood], but they are mighty before God for the overthrow and destruction of stronghold"*

sing to the Lord. I sang of His love, mercy, goodness, and grace. I sang of His victory and of the joy and peace He has given me. The more I sang, the more I felt like singing. I got louder and eventually His strength bubbled into joy. I began to laugh and the darkness broke. Depression, hurt, insecurity, and the rest of that crew left defeated.

And just like the Forrest Gump scene where the kids are on the school bus, in my best southern drawl, I said out loud, "Devil, you can't sit here, this seat's taken!" I chuckled to myself and moved on.

I got up from praying, dried my eyes and wiped my face, and pulled myself together. Another battle, another win. I talked to my husband and we got ourselves back on the same page. I later also told him what was going on with the brain fog so that I wouldn't carry that baggage in secret anymore either.

Life will happen. There will be days where it all seems to go south. Those are not the times to go it alone. Stay partnered with the Holy Spirit. Let Him teach you how to fight and how to use your weapons.

"For the weapons of our warfare are not physical [weapons of flesh and blood], but they are mighty before God for the overthrow and destruction of stronghold" (2 Corinthians 10:4 AMP). He instructs us what the weapons are, how to use them, and when. Sometimes He leads me to use the Word of God as a weapon, other times it's praying in the spirit. He is the Spirit of Truth and He wants to teach us how to be skillful in our praying and our fighting. Just like you don't bring knives to a gunfight, nor do you shoot bullets at flies, knowing what to use when makes all the difference. ⚬

"Humility of the heart creates an environment in which the Holy Spirit can thrive."

11

Pray 'til He Prays

A.W. Tozier's sermon, "Pray 'til you pray," references Dr. Moody Stuart's own personal rules of prayer. The one Tozier speaks of in his sermon is "pray 'til you pray." It's a good sermon to read if you haven't before, but in this chapter, we are taking that a step further. It's my personal rule of prayer that I refer to as the master key. Are you ready? Pray 'til He prays through you.

ISAIAH 59:19
*So shall they fear
The name of the Lord
from the west, And His
glory from the rising of
the sun; When the enemy
comes in like a flood,
The Spirit of the Lord
will lift up a standard
against him.*

Let me give you an example of what I mean.

It seemed like the rain had specifically come to challenge us that day. A hurricane had formed in the Gulf of Mexico some 400 miles away, but the storm surge had already extended into our area. As we began our Sunday worship service that morning, buckets of rain came down. Somehow our drainage system at church had gone bad and instead of the water draining off the rood onto the ground, it was being redirected inside, directly into the building and onto the lobby floor. The harder it rained, the more water came in. Right there, in the middle of singing praises to God, the church lobby flooded. Church members sprang into action. A symphony of Shop-Vacs, mops, and squeegees worked in harmony to keep the flood from reaching the sanctuary. When my husband walked into the lobby, an elder said, "We've got this pastor, you go preach the Word!"

The pastor walked back in the sanctuary not sure what to do with the physical situation out there, but he knew exactly what to do with the spiritual situation. Right there in the middle of the storm, he led the congregation into a praise and worship service with a fire and intensity that declared war in the Heaven-lies. We sang songs of thanksgiving and praise to the Almighty God. We lifted up the name of Jesus above every situation and circumstance. We danced like David did in the Old Testament. And as we worshiped, it was as if we saw the pastor living out what the prophet Isaiah said in the book of Isaiah 59:19, "... When the enemy shall come in like a flood, the Spirit of the Lord shall lift up a standard against him." A standard was indeed lifted, the presence of the Lord was so intense that we praised and worshiped the entire service.

With inches to spare, the rain stopped, and the water never made it into the sanctuary. Once the water was off the floor, everyone joined in to celebrate the victory we had through Jesus.

Victory, Angela? Yes, victory.

You see, on that particular day a baby dedication was scheduled and there were more visitors than usual. Now, it's one thing to have a water leak at the church when visitors come, but it's something quite different to have visitors literally wading through water in their Sunday best to get into the sanctuary. I know the pastor, my husband, had to be fighting against embarrassment and anger at the situation. Who wouldn't? But instead of panicking, instead of being consumed by the situation, he surrendered it to the Lord and the Lord used him mightily that day. The Lord used him to teach us how to handle those flood-like moments in our own personal lives. Not only do we keep praising, but we praise harder. Not only do we keep worshiping, but we worship deeper. We offer up thanksgiving from our hearts for all the Lord has done for us. And in that, we ensure that the enemy gets no satisfaction from the situation. Many of us in church that day needed to see an example of how to do just that. We needed to see how to walk in victory right in the middle of the storm.

After service was over and everyone left, my husband and I still had a lot of work to do. The water was out but the carpet was still soaking wet. We knew that was just the first wave of storms scheduled to come through. The hurricane was causing a series of tropical storms to come through. So, we got food, changed clothes, and came back up to the church to get to work.

To compound the situation, it was a holiday weekend. No contractors would be available for a couple of days. We rented a commercial grade carpet cleaner and patiently, methodically vacuumed the water out of the carpet, getting it dry and back to normal. But after about two hours, we heard the rain again. And then came the second flood.

This time we didn't have ten church members working together to help. It was just the two of us — oh, and our twins, who could only marvel at all the water coming into our lobby floor and of course want to play in it.

We couldn't keep it from coming in. It was incredible. We had no idea what to do or how to do it. Eric yelled, "Grab the squeegee and we will push it out!" I ran and we pushed. And we pushed. It seemed like with every push of the water out the door, that much more had come in. But we kept at it. We had no choice. When he got tired, I pushed. And right when we felt like giving up, we found we still had the energy to keep pushing. And we called on the Lord to help. He cried out, I cried out. "Lord, help us! Jesus, we need Your help! We don't know what to do, we don't know what to pray! But You see us down here! This is Your house." I was praying, listening intently for what the Holy Spirit was saying to pray.

I was praying until He prayed. I simply prayed, "Jesus, we need Your help." I could have flung out a series of "Christianese" phrases. I was tempted to declare and decree the victory we have in Jesus and quote scripture until I was blue in the face. But now wasn't the time for "hitting and missing," hoping I lucked up on the right words of faith. We needed the tropical storm to move from over our heads before the water spread through the entire building and only the Lord's word had power to do that.

As I prayed, listened, and pushed water out the door, I heard the Holy Spirit remind me of God's Word, remind me of who God is to us, remind me that it was just water. Through the frustration and overwhelm, I reminded my husband that we've been through much worse than a flooded lobby. I reminded him that we were not going to give up this fight just because we didn't know what to do. We were going to do what we knew to do until the Lord told us to do something different. Right now, we pray, and we push!

Encouraged, my husband took the squeegee back from me and kept moving the water out the door. And that's when I began to really pray. I told my mind to take a back seat and began to pray from my spirit thanking Him for all that He had already brought us through. I began to praise Him because I knew this time would be no different. I prayed until the He prayed through me. Until the Holy Spirit gave me the words of prayer.

"In prayer, expect to experience the power of God."

After a few minutes, I began saying out loud and with intensity, "Holy Father! You are the same God who split the Red Sea... Split this storm!" My husband stopped mid-stride, looked at me, and said, "Ah, that's it right there!" In that moment, those words confirmed in His spirit that those were the words of faith and the will of the Lord.

The presence of the Lord rested on me in that moment and I began to praise and pray in my heavenly language with great joy! Those were the words from heaven that we needed and had been waiting for. Literally, in less than three minutes, the rain stopped and the storm passed. We pushed the rest of the water out the door and began walking in faith in what the Lord had spoken.

When we were done, we got out our phones and looked at the weather apps to see the radar. It was incredible what we saw happen. We watched the green, yellow, and red bubbles that indicate where the rain was moving and the level of intensity dissolve around our area! We literally saw the predicted forecast change over time and what was a solid yellow and red area break into two, splitting as it neared Huntsville. We saw the rain chances go from 100 percent down to 35 percent and then 15 percent. We were in the clear for the rest of the night!

With that, faith and heads held high, we packed it up and went home. We would deal with the wet carpet in the morning. It was about 10:00 pm and that was enough for one day. That storm wave passed, but the weather forecast was still predicting a solid week of rain due to hurricane Alberto making its way up the coast.

COLOSSIANS 3:15
so if anyone of you is lacking in wisdom, let him keep asking god, for he gives generously to all and without reproaching, and it will be given him.

We continued talking about what had happened and the word of the Lord that caused the storm to split. We stood in awe and thanksgiving that the I AM had sent us His word and moved on our behalf.

This was May 27, 2018. The tropical storm that resulted from Hurricane Alberto continued to move over Alabama and it continued to split over our area in Huntsville, Alabama. If you want to see how the weather behaved, look up the historical radar data.

That's an example of the power and effectiveness of praying until He prays through you.

Isaiah says, "So shall My word be that goes forth from My mouth; It shall not return to Me void, But it shall accomplish what I please, And it shall prosper in the thing for which I sent it."

This kind of prayer causes storms to change course. It is prayer that results in the hand of God working on your behalf. Prayer that draws you into closer fellowship with the true and living God. This is the kind of prayer we have access to and the kind of prayer that will cause you to walk in victory every day of your life. This is praying to win. This is our master key.

You too can pray until He prays! The culmination of all the keys together are surmised in that one phrase. When you spend time, obey, believe, thank, praise, worship, surrender, forgive, remember, are honest, and all the other keys, your walk with Him will grow to where you hear the voice of the Lord directing even what you pray.

Jesus did this. He said, "I only do what I see the Father do." In another verse He said, "I only say what I hear the Father say." He does the work. Jesus showed us what a life of prayer not only sounded like in words, but what it looked like lived out. When we follow His living example, He promises to give us the results.

"If you abide in Me, and my words abide in you, you can ask what you will..." Why? Because His will becomes our will and our will becomes His. Isn't that beautiful? Isn't that miraculous?

"Do you see what this means—all these pioneers
who blazed the way, all these veterans cheering us
on? It means we'd better get on with it. Strip down,
start running—and never quit!"
HEBREWS 12:1 MSG

12

Every Time We Pray, We Win!

Put one foot in front of the other and pray. One of my daughters is prone to over-analyze activities that intimidate her. To get her in the right frame of mind I tell her, "You remember when you first started shooting basketball? Did you make the first shot? Or even the second?" She shyly smiles, recalling that. "And now you're one of the best players on your team, right?" She smiles. I personally think she's the best on the team period, but I'm her mom and that's my job. "How did you get there? By showing up and practicing. The more your practiced, the better you got, right? This is no different, it may seem challenging at first, but just try, just practice what you've been taught."

If prayer seems challenging to you, just practice what you've learned. And when you don't feel like it, do it anyway. I guarantee you won't always feel like it. I don't always feel like it. But what I know is that every time I pray, I win.

In some way I win. Whether it is in forging ahead in spiritual warfare, getting to know God and myself more, or by knowing that God hears my prayers and answers me, **I'M WINNING!**

When I pray about my marriage, **I'M WINNING**

When I pray about my career, **I'M WINNING**

When I pray about my family, **I'M WINNING**

When I pray for my church, **I'M WINNING**

When I pray for other people,
I'm #winningevenmore.

When I pray just to be in the Lord's presence,
I'm #winningthemost.

Every moment we spend before the Lord, something happens. Whether it be a change in our hearts, in our lives, in those we are praying for, whatever it is, something happens. Sometimes we can sense it right away, sometimes it may take a moment, sometimes we may never see it with our natural eyes, but something happens. We pray with intention, we pray with determination, we pray with confidence.

"And this is the confidence (the assurance, the privilege of boldness) which we have in Him: [we are sure] that if we ask anything (make any request) according to His will (in agreement with His own plan), He listens to and hears us.

And if (since) we [positively] know that He listens to us in whatever we ask, we also know [with settled and absolute knowledge] that we have [granted us as our present possessions] the requests made of Him."
1 JOHN 5:14-15 AMPC

Our prayers are more than vapors of hope. When we pray, we should have a certain swagger about it. Like, "My Daddy owns all of this and I know He loves me. So just as soon as I talk to Him, I already know everything is going to be alright."

My family hasn't taken many vacations. Pastoring a church is a 24/7 position and takes quite a bit of coordination, and most importantly, it takes the Lord's presence and His approval—it does for us, at least. When I recently had the opportunity to go with the family to Orlando, Florida on a work-related trip, I was super excited. We had never gone as a family and the twins were beyond excited—taking a week off school was a bonus all by itself.

The night before we were to drive down, the storms rolled in. If you recall in an earlier chapter that when it rains heavily, our church lobby would get water pouring in on the floor. Well, sure enough, it started again and on this particular night, the night right before we were supposed to leave town, we were eating dinner when a phone call came in. The alarm company said the church alarm had just gone off. Eric was sure nobody was trying to break into the church at 7 pm in the middle of the rain, but the motion sensor had gone off and the security team advised him to come.

We arrived with police officers in the parking lot. We didn't have an intruder, the ceiling tile had gotten so wet from the rain coming inside that it fell onto the ground, causing the sensors to trigger. When we looked at the floor, water was everywhere. Everywhere. In that moment, I just felt my heart sink.

I was used to working with my husband to vacuum the water up when it rained hard, but this week, we were going to be out of town and there was no way we could leave water standing in the church while we were gone. The weather forecast said to expect storms all week. Our hearts wouldn't let us enjoy a minute of our vacation knowing the mess we were leaving behind. That meant, in my mind, that the trip was off. To make matters worse, it was a work trip I had to attend but it was too late for me to book airfare, not at a price the company would pay for anyway. I was going to have to drive 11 hours all by myself. Oh, what a sad, sad look I had on my face. How would we explain this to the girls?

The police left. Eric, myself, and the kids drove home to change clothes, so we could get to work. I was quiet, my mind and my spirit fighting. My mind was going down all the scenarios of how bad of a week I was looking at. My inner spirit was reminding me that Jesus has the final say. I felt like the rug had just been pulled from underneath me and I was recalling to myself, Didn't the Lord approve this trip? He wouldn't set me up like this, I know He wouldn't. But it sure was looking that way.

We got home, changed clothes, and I sat at the top of the stairs for a minute. I was too upset to even cry. Finally, I came to my senses and prayed, "Lord, I know you have all the answers." Sometimes you have to fight against your feelings to get words of faith out. But be sure to get them out! Heaven and hell are listening, waiting to hear what it is you are going to say in response. What are you going to say? I came downstairs and Eric said, "Don't worry, the Lord is moving on your behalf."

I agreed with my spirit, but my mind was still at a loss on what to do. So I did what I knew to do, I got in the car to go help clean up until the Lord directed us further. Living by what He taught me, I did what I knew to do until He told me to do something different.

As we pulled into the church parking lot, we saw two cars already there. It was two of our elders already working to get the water up. We hadn't called a single person. We hadn't told anyone anything.

When we got inside they looked at us confused and said, "We thought you guys were gone already. With the way this rain is coming down, we figured we should come look after the church. When we saw all this water and mess, we just got to work."

Eric looked at me and just smiled. My heart sprung off the floor! Maybe, just maybe, the trip isn't off after all, I thought. My husband and I got out the other equipment and started helping. And then two more members came in! It was almost 9 pm and I knew these people had to work in the morning. But there they were, ready to help! "We're in this together, you guys go on your trip, we got this," they said cheerfully.

My heart went from floor to mountain top. The Lord had called people out of their homes, even out of their beds, to come help us that night. They wanted to make sure we knew we could leave in peace and everything would be taken care of.

Eric put everything back in place and we left the next day as planned. That was on a Tuesday. Wednesday came and it was raining so hard the lights went out. I knew because our house alarm sent me a text that the power had gone out. We were in sunny Florida, but Eric and I tossed and turned and prayed all night as it rained back home.

But on Thursday afternoon, we got a call from one of the elders. Not only had they managed to get all the water up again from the storm, but in the middle of the buckets of rain, the contractors we had been waiting on for weeks finally showed up! They scaled the roof in the rain, fixed the drainage issue, and the water leak stopped immediately. Not one more drop came in. It was fixed! That news alone was like a whole new vacation! We celebrated and enjoyed the rest of our vacation like we didn't have a care in the world! The church was fixed!

Not only did God save my vacation, He fixed an issue we had been battling with for months. Elated, Eric and I immediately began planning how to redo the lobby. Now that the water leak issue was fixed, we could begin restoring the Lord's house. That was like a vacation on top of a vacation!

We all have flooded lobbies in our lives. Battles we face that seem bigger than ourselves. During those times, it's rarely easy to take the position of confidence in God, but let me strongly encourage you to do just that. He is true to His word. When we walk in fellowship through prayer and obedience in life, we can be assured to live in His blessings. Prayer and obedience is a lifestyle, and a highly profitable one at that. ⊙➤

It is my prayer and expectation that what we have covered in this book will be put into practice and will cause a new level of power and effectiveness in your prayer life and in your Christian walk. Here's a recap of what we've learned:

01.   Know why you pray.

02.   Be honest with yourself and God in prayer.

03.   Obedience is where the rubber meets the road.We can talk it, but it won't work until we walk it.

04.   The name of Jesus reflects the character and authority of God. Praying in that name enables us to pray with His power.

05.   Thanksgiving is the password. Don't forget to use it.

06.   Believe! Doubt profits nothing.

07.   There is no substitute for time. There is no microwave relationship with God. Settle in and enjoy the journey.

08.   Persist! Always, persist.

09.   Practice allowing the Holy Spirit to lead you. Partner with Him.

10.   Pray until the Holy Spirit gives you what to pray. Listen, then speak.

Finally, "... whatever you do in word or deed, do all in the name of the Lord Jesus, giving thanks to God and the Father by Him."

COLOSSIANS 3:17

AMEN!

Jesus came and said to them:
All authority in heaven and on earth
has been given to Me. Therefore go and
make disciples of all nations. Matthew
28:18

Christ Jesus said Behold I give unto you
power to tread on serpents and scorpions
and over All the power of the enemy;
and NOTHING shall by any means hurt
you. Luke 10:19

Made in the USA
Coppell, TX
23 May 2023

17206507R00079